LIVE, DIE,
and
TAKE NOTES

Discovering Other Worlds and the Purpose
of Living through Past Life Regressions

Anat Weinstein

HIGHER CHOICE PUBLISHING

Library of Congress Control Number: 2015915387

ISBN 978-0-9963791-0-6

First Printing, 2015

Cover Design Copyright © 2015
by (http://DigitalDonna.Com)

Higher Choice Publishing
PO Box 53291
Albuquerque, NM 87153
www.NMhypnosis.com

Table of Contents

INTRODUCTION

O NE DAY I woke up from my life. I woke up the same way you suddenly realize, late in the afternoon, that you have been watching TV for so long that there is not much left of the day.

I was in my mid-thirties. I looked at my life and saw that I had spent it all on the story of myself. And I realized that there had to be more to life than that. At that time I was in the habit of spending about eight hours every day in a cubicle, working as a mechanical engineer. The economy was going downhill, and the company I was working for did not have many projects to work on. As a result, I spent many hours each day in that cubicle without much work to do — at least not the kind I was supposed to get paid for. I had a lot of free time to think. For whatever reason, my mind chose to focus on the mystery of existence. I kept asking myself: *Why am I here? Why am I alive? What is life, anyway?*

In an attempt to find answers, I did what I usually do to find information: I googled "the meaning of life." I did not find any satisfactory answers that way. Looking into religious materials did not even cross my mind. I grew up in Israel, where there is no separation between state and religion. I had to study the Old Testament at school, but it never made sense to me. I found too many contradictions in it and could not believe in a violent and vengeful God. I then proceeded to read about Einstein's Theory of Relativity. According to that theory, time does not actually exist, and if time does not exist that means space does not exist either. As Einstein famously put it: "Reality is an illusion, albeit a very persistent one."

From there it was easy to deduce that I did not exist and neither did Descartes. He only *thought* he did. But what did all this mean? I felt as if a deep part of me knew the answers, but somehow I was unable to reach them. I felt as if I had amnesia, as if I did know but could not remember. Then the idea of hypnosis came to mind. I did not know much about hypnosis, but I thought it was a way to remember things that had been forgotten. I ordered a couple of books about self-hypnosis online.

Increasingly obsessed with the meaning of life, I kept asking myself: Who am I? I felt that because I could not remember why I was here on earth, I could not know who I was. I am not my name; I am not my memories; I am not my job. I am not even my thoughts or my emotions. Finally, I am not my body. *Then who am I?*

I had tried discussing these issues with a few friends, but no one seemed to care. The topic did not seem to hold anyone's interest but mine. While other people seemed to be busy with their day-to-day lives, I was consumed by the absence of apparent meaning in life. I continued to go to work and participate absent-mindedly in my everyday life, but my heart and my mind were elsewhere.

Even though I perceived myself as an atheist, I found myself bargaining with some higher power I did not even believe existed. I made a list of all the things I was willing to give up in order to know the Truth: my money, my job, my friends, and my life. If I had been convinced that by ending my life I would get to the bottom of it, I would have ended it. I was not depressed or suicidal, only determined. I started to make vague threats to no one in particular: if someone did not show up and explain to me exactly why I was supposed to get up every morning and play my role in a script I had never agreed to, I would just stop. I would not participate in life anymore. I would stay home and not move or make a sound until I understood. *That's it*, I thought, *I'll quit.* I was pretty sure, however, that this kind of "quitting" would end up with me in a straitjacket somewhere. Not an appealing thought!

This went on for a while. Then somehow, without me even realizing it at first, my cry for help was answered.

My journey to discover the Truth began over ten years ago. This is not the story of that incredible journey. This is about other stories, stories that are parts of the Truth I was seeking.

As it happened, I never did read those books about self-hypnosis that I ordered. But more than three years later I started to study hypnosis and got professional training.

Now I use hypnosis to search and find my answers. They might not be everyone's answers, but they mean a lot to me. They mean so much to me that I feel compelled to share them. If there are other people out there who are seeking, I hope they will find this book worth reading. And those who are not seeking might find it interesting as well. Sometimes people search even though they don't consciously know it.

Several years ago I finally walked away from my old life as an engineer. I'd become a mechanical engineer because I was always fascinated with physics; I always wanted to know how things worked. As soon as I realized that physics and the laws of nature might be only localized phenomena determined by our limited perceptions, I had to enlarge my viewpoint of life and reality. In the process, science lost most of its appeal. Instead of being curious about *how* things work, I needed to know *why*.

The question of *why* opened a door to a new world for me: the spiritual realm.

I became fascinated with past life regressions. I wanted to know everything there was to know about reincarnation and the world beyond the physical realm. I use hypnosis to gather information and find answers to many questions.

One of the most fascinating sources of information came from an unexpected source: a person I have known most of my life, who wishes to remain anonymous. We will call him Ben.

I was born and grew up in Israel. I live in New Mexico, USA. On one of Ben's visits here, I asked him if he wanted to try a past life regression. I needed the practice, I told him. I had just learned a new technique I wanted to try. Ben was an engineer. He had no knowledge or exposure to New Age ideas or any background in spirituality. He agreed to try, but said he didn't know if he believed in reincarnation and expressed doubts that he would be a good candidate to practice on. We decided to try anyway.

In our first session, he went back to a life as a Viking. I kept that session simple and did not ask many questions. After that session, Ben said that he didn't know if he made that life up or if it was real; perhaps he'd concocted it from ideas and images from movies or TV.

My opinion was that it didn't matter. As long as he received useful information from the session, the experience had value.

Since that session seemed to be a success, we decided to do more. In the second session, I was astounded by what he came up with. After that, I couldn't leave him alone. I kept asking him to do more and more sessions. The sessions in this book were conducted over the course of five years. To this day, he says that he is not sure whether he made it all up or if it was real.

It is not my intention to prove that reincarnation is real. There are other books about that. In this book the focus is not only on other lives, other worlds, or on the idea that we never really die. The content reveals a broader perspective on reality and life than we are normally aware of. Our world, as we experience it, is inundated with injustice and chaos. The same world, viewed from a larger perspective, can be better understood. In this book, stories about different experiences are used to impart lessons about life, consciousness, and the purpose of living. It is my intention to share these powerful ideas, so they will inspire you and enable you to live a better and happier life. These ideas and lessons just happened to surface in past life regressions.

The sessions in this book are in chronological order and have been translated from Hebrew. There are a few omissions from the original transcripts, mostly personal information that would be of no interest to the reader.

I have decided to present the sessions as they are and not include too many of my own personal interpretations or ideas. I believe it would be best for readers to relate to the ideas in their own way and let the messages speak directly to them. I see the sessions as works of art or poetry, and therefore it is not my place to offer explanations. At the end of each session, however, I do offer a brief commentary and a few questions, in the style of a study guide that may help you deepen your understanding of what you've read, and how it might relate to your own life. I also offer a few affirmations that are related to the sessions in the hope they may help you implement some of the ideas presented.

It is my sincere hope that if you happened to pick up this book, it would speak to your heart just as the revelations in the sessions spoke to mine.

ABOUT REINCARNATION

When the physical body dies, the consciousness that inhabited it continues to exist and moves on to a different physical existence, a reincarnation.

Different religions teach different versions of this concept. Some believe that consciousness, or the soul, always reincarnates as a human being. Others believe that the soul can also experience existences as animals or plants.

According to some traditions, the type of body that the soul is assigned to is determined by *karma* defined as the sum of a being's actions in this and previous states of existence. It speaks of progression from lower forms of existence (plants for example) to animals and then humans. The better the karma, the higher level of existence the soul experiences.

Belief in reincarnation is widespread in the East. It is increasingly more popular in the West in recent years, and many popular books have been written on the subject.

According to the sessions in this book, the soul's incarnations are not limited to human lives, animals, plants or even to existence on Earth. This striking aspect of these sessions reveals a broader cosmic vision of consciousness.

ABOUT PAST LIFE REGRESSION

In a past life regression, an altered state of consciousness is induced using hypnosis techniques. The person is then guided to relive experiences from past lives. The idea is that we all have a part of us that remembers our experiences in different incarnations. For most people, the conscious mind only remembers experiences from their current lives. In order to remember a past life, a different state of awareness has to be experienced. In an altered state, deeper parts of consciousness become more accessible and memories from different incarnations can be recalled. The awareness of the current life might still be present to varying degrees and affect the perception and interpretation of past life information. The person going through a recollection of a past life, experiences the events and information mostly through the perspective of the consciousness he identifies with at the time. I chose to leave the stories as they were originally told and not modify them to better fit into a modern "politically correct" worldview. It is important to clarify that it is not the intention of this book to offend anyone on the grounds of race, gender, social status, or anything else. According to the information presented in the sessions, we all take turns in living and being anything and everything that exist anyway. We are all one consciousness.

In the sessions presented in this book, I used various techniques of inducing hypnosis and facilitating recollections of past lives.

Every session except the first one is divided into two parts. The first part is the recollection of past lives. In the second part of the session, I speak to the part of the consciousness that is aware of all the lives the soul experienced, asking for explanations and interpretations. Whether or not one believes in reincarnation, the lessons drawn from these various experiences are significant and useful.

SESSION ONE

A Viking without Conscience

THIS is the first session I had with Ben. At this point I was "testing the waters" to see if he would come up with any past life at all. Thus I kept the session simple and did not ask many questions.

Ben: I am a man, about thirty years old. I have light skin and long brown hair. I'm wearing a fur coat, fur shoes and carrying a shield and a sword. It seems I'm a Viking. There are other people watching me and working. We're sailing on a Viking ship. It is medium size, like a large yacht. I am in control. I am the commander.

Anat: Move forward in time to a significant event in that life.

B: It is nighttime. I'm on land with my people. We are conquering a village. There are many screams of women and children. There are fires all around. I feel indifferent; this seems normal.

A: Move forward in time to the next significant event in that life.

B: I'm in a government building. There is a trial for what I did, for the pillaging. I feel indifferent. I don't understand why they judge, what the problem with that is.

A: How is the trial conducted? Do you have a lawyer?

B: No. It's only me and five people in front of me, asking questions. They're asking why I did what I did. I'm saying that's what I thought had to be done. They are saying that there are proper ways to do things and that is not the way.

A: And how do you feel about what's happening?

B: Indifferent. I can't connect with my feelings. I seem to realize that this is not the way, and I understand I have a problem in the brain; I have no conscience. I'm afraid of the verdict.

A: Move forward in time to the outcome of the trial and tell me what was decided at the end.

B: It was decided to send me to prison for ten years.

A: *How do you feel about that?*

B: Not good. I understand that the punishment is appropriate, but it's as if I don't deserve it. I don't have control over who I am. The 'I' that does things is actually not me. It's only my actions; it's not me. As if I'm not responsible for my actions because I was created without willpower. I do things for no reason and not because I want to. I feel some disconnection between me and myself. Like I'm not a man, like I'm an animal triggered by instincts. I feel there is no point to life.

A: *Move forward to the next significant event in that life.*

B: I'm about sixty years old. I'm wearing simple work clothes. I'm helping people build houses. I feel good about it.

A: *Are you friends with those people?*

B: No, I'm not. I'm just helping them.

A: *Do you get anything in return?*

B: No.

A: *What is important to know about this event?*

B: I'm still disconnected from myself. I'm helping them not because I want to. It's a kind of atonement for what happened. Like I'm still not connected to what I want.

A: *Move forward in time to the events that lead up to your death in that life.*

B: I'm ninety years old. I'm with my wife and a doctor. I have pneumonia because it is very cold.

A: *How do you feel about your wife?*

B: I love her.

A: *Move forward to the last moments of that life and connect to your thoughts and feelings.*

B: I feel my life was wasted. I was in prison, and I was indifferent. I felt like an animal, unsatisfied with my life.

A: *What decisions are you making now about yourself or about life in general?*

B: That I have to do soul searching, to find myself, instead of acting like a robot or like an animal. I decide not to hurt anyone anymore. I'm glad to die because I no longer have to be who I am.

A: *After you leave your body, become aware of all the important information you need to know.*

B: I'm being shown all that I did, all the bad things I did. I cannot understand why I did evil. I feel like I was destined to do evil. As if I was destined to not be aware of myself, not be connected to myself.

A: *Find out why you had to experience that. What was the lesson?*

B: To show me that when you don't take control, everything is bad. Then you're not a man anymore.

A: *Control — you mean, taking responsibility for your actions?*

B: Yes.

A: *How is that life affecting you now?*

B: I still feel disconnected, not in control, like a leaf floating in the river.

A: *How can you change that in your present life?*

B: Try to make decisions.

A: *Is this the lesson from that life that is relevant to your current life?*

B: Maybe, but I feel there is something else, but I can't seem to know what it is.

A: *Connect to the knowledge again. What was the lesson in that life?*

B: I think to know myself. To know what I am, who I am, and what I want.

A: *Find out what you're supposed to do in this present life.*

B: Perhaps more meditation, listen to myself more, do external things less and be more creative.

A: *How to be creative, for example?*

B: Draw.

A: *How do you feel about these things? Do you want to do them?*

B: Yes.

COMMENTARY

This session describes a life as a Viking without conscience or compassion. He was disconnected from his feelings and thus did not assume responsibility for his actions. He did not understand his own motivations and felt that his life was not worth living if he did not know himself and was driven purely by instincts.

MESSAGES

1. When one does not take responsibility for one's actions, there are consequences.
2. To know oneself is essential to fulfillment in life.

STUDY QUESTIONS

1. Are you in touch with your own feelings enough to feel compassion for others?
2. What helps you to connect to yourself and know yourself better?

AFFIRMATIONS

1. Because I take responsibility for my actions, I am constantly learning and growing.
2. Because I love and accept myself completely, I do good and kind things for others.

SESSION TWO

The Colorful Planet

AFTER a successful first attempt at a past life regression, I decided to try a technique I had learned from Dolores Cannon. After a person experiences a past life, she asks to speak to what she calls the "subconscious," although that level of awareness may actually be what some people refer to as the "superconscious mind" or the "higher self."

With Cannon's technique, the person writes down a list of questions ahead of time, focusing on any issues they might be struggling with, from health, to relationships, career, or even life's purpose. By writing down these questions, people give the subconscious mind a direction toward which past life would be most beneficial for them to explore. After exploring the past life, the hypnotherapist calls forward the subconscious and asks the list of questions the person came up with.

This is the first session I had with Ben in which he wrote down questions, and then I asked his subconscious mind to come up with answers.

One of the issues he wanted to ask about was a lump in his body that a physician had said might be cancer — but there was no way to know until he had surgery to remove it. He had to wait a couple of weeks until the surgery and experienced great distress and fear during that time. The surgery revealed that the lump was a hernia, and he was otherwise healthy.

About a year later, he again had a lump and had to go through the whole ordeal again, with the same result. So he wanted to know why he had to go through those experiences. Further questions appear in the session. While I was focusing during the session on asking the right questions and trying to understand his descriptions, it was not until afterward that I realized I had received answers to my most nagging questions: why are we here on Earth, and where did we come from?

Ben: I am on a different planet. It looks very colorful, like plasticine with lots of colors, colored stripes. The entire planet is kind of half-liquid, half-solid. I'm standing, and I'm a part of the planet; I'm a being that is merged with the planet. I'm also very colorful, and all the beings are protrusions of the planet. My body is part of the planet, connected to the planet.

Anat: How do you move?

B: I have legs? Not legs... I'm moving like someone who is connected to the ground, but still moves, while merged with the ground.

A: What are you doing there on the planet? What do people do?

B: Moving with the planet all the time. I don't see any houses or anything like that. I only see a huge surface of colors, mixed together. Everyone is moving. After pausing next to each other, we continue moving on.

A: What happens when you stop next to each other? Do you communicate with one another?

B: There's some type of communication. Perhaps telepathy...

A: Do you know the other people? Do you have any relationships with them?

B: No relationships. They all seem the same size. Everyone is actually a mixture of colors.

A: How are you feeling?

B: I think I like it here. I feel good and always in motion. Moving all the time and looking for interactions, talking to people, being next to someone else, exchanging information, and then moving on.

A: What type of information do you exchange?

B: I'm stopping next to someone, a being. The being is a part of the planet. He's telling me about life on other planets. He's been to other planets, and he's telling me about others who have been to other planets. I envy him because I haven't been to other planets yet, and I want to.

A: *How can you make it happen?*

B: When I look around, I see other figures disconnecting from the planet like missiles. Not everyone is able to disconnect. Some try a little, but only a little. Their connection with the ground becomes narrower, like rubber or chewing gum, but they don't succeed.

A: *What determines whether they succeed or not?*

B: It depends on willpower and the readiness of that being to disconnect.

A: *Move forward to a point in time when you manage to disconnect from the planet.*

B: I finally succeed after trying for a very long time. It was hard. After I disconnect, I'm beginning to fly up very slowly. I fly up into space and see other beings flying around me. They are also from the planet, but they are not with me. Each one flies his own course, not in groups. There are no groups. Each one is alone. I'm flying, and I see all kinds of planets above, and I need to decide where to fly. There are a variety of planets in different colors. I'm taking my time. I'm simply flying. I feel good because I'm going to see new things after a long time.

A: *Move forward in time until you choose a planet.*

B: I choose a light colored planet. It is the color of sand, like a desert, but not as hot as a desert. I reach the planet and land there, but no one can see me. I don't know why, but no one sees me, while I see other beings. All kinds of people... not people, but we'll call them people. They are all brown, like sticks. Their bodies resemble human bodies, but they are longer, taller and thinner. They are not wearing clothes. There are others, animals with four legs, and the people are hitting them to make them work. The animals are like slaves. I feel very bad about the animals. Why are the people hitting them? The brown people are evil.

A: *What are you doing?*

B: Nothing. I can't do anything. I have no physical interaction with this place. I'm like a ghost. I'm staying there for a while.

A: *Move forward in time until you decide to leave.*

B: I decide to fly away from the planet. It's easy to fly away from here. I'm not connected. No willpower is required. I'm flying up.

Everything is black and there are stars. It's difficult to decide whether to continue to another planet or return to mine.

A: *Can you find your own planet and return to it if you want to?*

B: Yes, because it's always visible, always colorful. I decide to return to my planet. I land and connect to the ground. I'm starting to go, to move. I'm meeting other beings, telling them about what I saw. I saw evil. I'm asking a being if all the planets are evil. The being tells me that they're not all evil, and that there are other types of planets. So I say that I want to see such a place, a good place. The being tells me how to get to such a place. I decide to go there, so I'm disconnecting from the planet again.

I'm flying up. I get to a planet where everything is a shade of blue. I land there. Again, I'm not physically connected to the planet. I'm only observing, and I see beings that look human. All the beings are pretty. They're talking and laughing. There are animals, and no one hurts the animals.

I feel that I want to live in a place like this. I want to experience it and experience more than just information.

A: *So, what happens?*

B: I can stay here on this planet, but I can't be a part of it. I can only observe. I'm not allowed to be a part of it because I'm a different type of being. I can only experience information, and I don't feel good about it.

A: *So what do you do?*

B: I decide to remain on that planet longer, to observe and to learn.

A: *Move forward in time until you are done observing and tell me what happens.*

B: I'm taking off and flying back to my planet. I land on the planet and tell others about what I saw, and how much I would like to be there. I'm told I cannot because I'm a different kind of being. I don't feel good about it because that's a place where I want to live, and I can't.

A: *Move forward in time until something significant happens, something that's related to your desire to live on that planet.*

B: After many, many years, I'm offered an option to die. They ask me if I want to die. If I die, I can become a being on the planet I liked. But if I die, I can no longer be myself, no longer who I am now. Everything I had experienced, everything I had observed, would all die with me. I would lose all the knowledge.

A: *Who offers you that?*

B: There are other beings like me, perhaps a bit larger than me.

A: *Then what happens?*

B: I tell them I've decided to die. They tell me that in order to die I have to sink into the planet. I have to enter the planet. So I do, and it takes a lot of willpower to sink into the planet and become absorbed. It feels like I'm falling asleep. After I fall asleep, I become a child on the blue planet.

A: *How do you feel?*

B: I feel good, like a normal child.

A: *Do you have any memories from the other planet?*

B: No, I don't. Everyone is blue. They look human, but they're blue.

A: *How is life there?*

B: Life is normal, good. People swim in the pool. We don't have jobs. We eat fruits and vegetables. Everyone is playing together. Nobody makes the other angry. Everybody is nice. We live in families of four or five people.

A: *Move forward in time to a significant event in that life on the blue planet.*

B: I'm looking at myself and I'm no longer blue.

A: *What color are you?*

B: I seem to be brown.

A: *Where are you? Are you still on the blue planet?*

B: I am on the blue planet, but I'm looking at my hands and they're turning brown. I don't understand why I'm brown while everyone else is blue. I'm afraid it's because I've had bad, unhappy thoughts. Maybe I'm not good. Maybe I'm not happy like everyone else, so I'm becoming brown, becoming evil. I don't know whether others notice that I'm turning brown. I don't see anything different in my environment.

A: *What thoughts do you have?*

B: I want to hurt other people, kill them... take things for myself...

A: *Do such things happen on that planet?*

B: No. Never. Not outwardly. I haven't seen anything like this before. Everyone is blue. I'm beginning to think that maybe there are other brown people, not blue, and I just don't see their true color. If I'm brown, there might be others. I don't know...

A: *Move forward in time to the last day of your life on the blue planet.*

B: I'm an old man. I have a family, grandchildren and great-grandchildren. It feels like I'm going to die.

A: *What color are you?*

B: Light blue, very light blue.

A: *How do you feel?*

B: I feel that I don't know the truth about my essence, about the other beings on the planet, about their true color. I'm not brown now. I'm very light blue, almost white. I don't know whether I'm good or evil.

A: *Move forward in time to the last few moments before you die. Tune into your thoughts and feelings and then tell me.*

B: I'm thinking that I want to get another chance to live on that planet and be blue the entire time. I think I was brown for a long time, many times, and that wasn't good. It's like I sinned, so I want another chance.

A: *Move forward in time to the moment you leave the physical body. What are your thoughts and feelings after you leave your body?*

B: I'm happy because I know I'll get another chance to be what I want to be.

A: *What happens after you leave your body?*

B: I go back to the colorful planet. I get reborn there by emerging from the ground like a bubble, and I become a colorful being again. I feel good because I know that all the options are open for me. I know I can experience whatever I want to.

A: *So what do you do? Are you staying there?*

B: For now I'm staying because I want to visit more planets, so that I can decide where I would like to live next.

A: *Move forward in time until you decide you want to live on Earth. What happens to make you choose Earth?*

B: After talking to other beings, I find out that there's a place called Earth, where it's possible to be all different colors. It's possible to experience it as well as observe it and gather information. Life there is not long, so when you die, you return to the colorful planet. I decide that I want to try it.

First, I fly there to see what it is, and what it's like there. By using a lot of willpower, I disconnect from the planet. I fly to Earth. I see all kinds of people, streets and buildings. Everyone is busy, shouting and laughing. I decide I want to live there at least for a short time on a trial basis, so I go back to the colorful planet and tell them I want to die. Then I simply die. I connect with the planet and sink into it. I become the planet. I feel as if I'm falling asleep. Then I find myself on Earth. I'm an Eskimo. Everything is white. I feel good. It's a little cold, but I feel alive, even though it's cold, snowy and white. I feel alive when I care for the dogs, and I go fishing.

A: *Do you have any memory of the other planet?*
B: No.

A: *May I speak with Ben's subconscious?*
B: Yes.
A: *Why did you choose to show Ben the colorful planet?*

Subconscious: To show him that everything is temporary, and you don't really die. You just do different things every time you live. There is much information in all the different lives. If you want, you can also experience lives instead of just collecting information. You can share information from these experiences and also experience things based on the experiences of others.

A: *Why is it important for him to understand it now?*

SC: So that he won't take things so hard. Everything is temporary. Everything is meant to be experienced and then turned into information, to show others that they can also have the experience if they want to. Whatever is experienced is temporary, so it should be taken lightly.

A: Why did you show him the light colored planet with the brown people, where he saw evil?

SC: The reason for that came later. The purpose was to show him that blue people could be brown people without anyone knowing. He knows what it means to be brown because he saw the brown people. If I had turned him into a brown being without first experiencing the brown planet, he wouldn't have known why he was brown. When he became brown, he realized he had evil thoughts. He now understands that a person may have both positive and negative traits.

A: Were the blue people really blue, or did they also have brown traits?

SC: Ben only saw himself as brown. He concluded that if he was brown then there were probably others who were brown, without his knowledge. He couldn't be certain, but in fact all the people are not only blue. They are also brown. It is impossible to know. A person, a being, cannot know that about another. Beings can only know about themselves. They can only speculate that others are brown.

A: Is the colorful planet his home? His source?

SC: The colorful planet is actually his base. It is the eternal place and eternal time he will always return to. He will be reborn inside the colorful planet and always receive information from other beings.

A: Does everyone have such a base?

SC: Everyone has a base. That is everyone's base actually.

A: The same planet?

SC: The same colorful planet. Yes.

A: So all the people here on Earth, they are all connected to the colorful planet?

SC: Yes.

A: What is the purpose of life here on Earth?

SC: The purpose is actually to be the brown planet and the blue planet at the same time and to see that sometimes other people are brown. On the blue planet, Ben couldn't see brown people, but on Earth he is able to see brown people and blue people and all the colors in between. He can deal with his own colors, his own brown, his own blue, and other people's brown and blue. He can experience and feel what it's like to be brown and to be blue, and what it's like to receive brown or blue from other people. What he saw on the brown planet and on the blue planet are two extremes. Here on Earth, there's less uncertainty because it's possible to see the brown and the blue of other people. In a sense, it's a little easier than on the blue planet because here it's possible to see the colors sometimes.

A: Why is it important to see the colors?

SC: Because one should know when one is receiving brown from someone. It is important to know how to handle and accept it and also know that it's all okay. Ben chooses how to perceive things. Whether he is given brown or blue, he should not take it so hard. He should be less preoccupied with what color other people are and focus on what happens when he receives certain colors, so he knows how to deal with them.

A: Why is that important?

SC: To make him feel better. Ben feels bad when he doesn't know how to deal with the colors he receives from outside.

A: So, is Ben's purpose in this life to feel good?

SC: The ultimate goal is to feel good, but the goal on Earth is to know how to make himself feel good.

A: Just before he died on the blue planet he was a different color: very light blue, almost white. What was the meaning of that?

SC: He looked at himself, and he didn't know whether he was good or bad; whether he was brown or blue. I made him that color so that he would want to know what color he is, feel all the colors and be on Earth in order to know his true color at any given time.

A: Is his true color the one he chooses to be?

SC: His color is ultimately whatever he chooses, but sometimes I select a color for him. Because I select it, he doesn't always understand the reason for that choice. I do it to help him learn the reason. He will have to search within himself for the understanding of why he is a specific color.

A: So this is actually a way to encourage him to do some soul searching?

SC: Yes, so that he will understand and know why I chose that specific color for him.

A: In the previous session we had, he saw a life as a Viking. Was that a real experience?

SC: Yes, it was.

A: Why did he see that life?

SC: Because he needs to see what it is like to be brown. He was on the brown planet, and he didn't like being there because he saw that everything was bad. There was slavery, and the beings were brown and evil. I let him be brown, completely brown, to experience what it's like to be brown. Sometimes, when you are brown, it is not because you want to, but because I want you to. This is done, so he can connect to himself better and to all the colors he can be.

A: Do you mean he should know why he is every color?

SC: Yes. Every time he experiences certain emotions, there is a reason for it. Sometimes the reason is to experience the color and its significance. There may be other reasons. When Ben doesn't do what he is supposed to, or he procrastinates, I make him feel bad. He may not know why he feels bad, but if he reaches deep within himself, he will realize he wasn't doing what he was supposed to. Certain things, like skipping exercise in the morning, for example, make him feel bad. If he doesn't have breakfast, then sometimes he will feel bad in the morning. He won't understand why he feels bad unless he makes a real effort thinking about it.

A: If he tries to understand, will you help him figure out the reason?

SC: Yes. If he asks questions, I will try to answer.

A: What would be a good way for him to ask questions and get answers?

SC: He should close his eyes and attempt to talk to me. He should meditate and listen to himself. He should make time for me.

A: Doesn't he make enough time for that?

SC: No. He doesn't make any time for that at all. Instead of making time to understand why he feels bad, he tries to feel good. He does this by using distractions. So he skips the understanding about the bad feeling. Instead of experiencing the bad feeling, he "goes to sleep" and doesn't try to understand why the bad feeling is there, or why I made him feel that way. It would serve him better to understand that he doesn't have to feel bad, and he doesn't need distractions in order to feel good.

A: So what's the best way to feel good?

SC: To understand why the feelings are there, or why I made him feel bad. He should seek to understand what causes me to make him feel that way.

A: About exercising... he had those surgeries for the hernia. He said that he is afraid to exercise because of it. Is there any reason not to exercise because of that?

SC: No. It is safe for him to exercise. There are no restrictions.

A: Why did the hernia and the surgeries happen to him?

SC: Because I wanted him to experience real fear. Ben is afraid of many things that are not real. He is afraid of a lot of things he imagines, so I wanted him to know real fear. So that he can distinguish between the real and the imaginary.

A: Why did he have to experience it twice?

SC: Because he still didn't understand after the first time.

A: And now?

SC: Now, he understands better.

A: Then he will not have to go through that again?

SC: (Laughing) I hope not...

A: Speaking of his body, he's been suffering from hemorrhoids for years now. What's the reason for that? Is there anything you can do about that, to make him heal?

SC: Yes. I can cure him. The hemorrhoids are there to remind him that he is not doing what he is supposed to. As long as he doesn't do what he is supposed to, the hemorrhoids will not go away.

A: When you say, "what he is supposed to" — can you be more specific?

SC: Whatever he has to do in order to talk to me or to connect with me; things like meditation and creative activities. As long as he remains in his current state, I will leave it as a physical reminder.

A: So this is a reminder to talk to you?

SC: Yes.

A: When he does what he is supposed to, like meditate, draw and try to connect with you more, will you heal him?

SC: Yes, I will.

A: He said that many times he feels a little anxious. For example, it might happen right before a meeting at work, before he interacts with people, when he has to do something new or change something. He said it happens a lot.

SC: Yes, sometimes Ben feels a slight anxiety. It is to let him know that it's time for him to get ready for the interaction. When Ben was on the colorful planet, everything was about the exchange of information between one being to another. So Ben wanted every interaction on Earth to be a feeling, unlike on the colorful planet. He wanted to experience the interaction. Somehow Ben translates it into a feeling of anxiety. He doesn't have to do that. It is simply a feeling, a feeling of interaction. He asked for it.

A: Can you help him to experience it as something other than anxiety, and perhaps more pleasant?

SC: Yes. I will help him with that.

A: I'm sure he will be glad to hear that. And the last question he wants to ask is: why is he so afraid of change?

SC: On the colorful planet it was very difficult for him to disconnect, even though he wanted to discover other worlds. He was afraid to die and wanted to stay somewhere on the colorful planet, so he retained some of that fear. He needed it to feel as if he did not die and was still connected to that planet. The fear of change on the colorful planet was simply reborn with him on the new planet, on Earth.

A: Then is it actually the fear of leaving that planet?

SC: Yes.

A: Is there any way you can help him now in this life, to leave that fear of change where it belongs, on that planet, so that he will not have that in this life or have less of it?

SC: Because this fear is strong in Ben, I can reduce it, yes. I will leave it on the colorful planet. I will help him.

A: In his session as a Viking, he said he felt emotionally disconnected. He still has the same feeling in this life. Is there anything you can do to help him with that?

SC: Ben is emotionally disconnected because he doesn't try to talk to me. As soon as he talks to me, he will connect emotionally.

A: Before I bring Ben back, do you have any messages for him?

SC: Yes. Take things lightly because everything is temporary.

A: Is that the most important thing?

SC: Yes.

A: Ok. Thank you...

COMMENTARY

In this session the colorful planet is introduced. It is described as the base everyone on Earth comes from. We venture off that base to other planets, so we can have different experiences and then report back. We choose the planets and the type of experiences we have. We temporarily lose our eternal perspective in favor of a very limited one in order to have specific experiences.

If every life is one of many and there is no real death, then our essence or awareness is never really in danger. We exist forever regardless of the "stories" we experience during our lifetimes. This understanding requires a major shift in our perspective on living and dying.

MESSAGES

1. Everything is temporary and there is no real death, so things should be taken lightly.
2. It is better to understand the cause of a bad feeling instead of trying to feel good by using distractions.
3. In order to feel emotionally connected in life, one needs to spend time connecting with the self through meditation and creative activities.

STUDY QUESTIONS

1. Do you often seek distractions in order to try to feel good, instead of seeking to understand the cause of your distress?
2. What creative activities help you feel connected?
3. Do you spend time in meditation or contemplation?

AFFIRMATIONS

1. My true essence is eternal and immortal; therefore I am always safe.
2. I am far greater than my personality or my life story; therefore I always have the strength to deal with anything that occurs in my life.
3. Because I spend time in meditation and contemplation, I have more and more control over the way I feel.

SESSION THREE

A Thief and a King

AFTER the fascinating descriptions from the last session, I looked forward to the next one; it was like reading a novel I couldn't put down. I kept telling Ben to go to the next place because I didn't want the session to end. Eventually he said, "I'm exhausted." I had to stop sending him places and get through his questions. We agreed that future explorations would end when he tired.

In accordance with Dolores Cannon's technique, Ben was told to visualize himself on a cloud. Then the cloud carried him to the past life he was seeking. He was reassured that when he was too tired, he could always return to the cloud. That would signal that it was time to conclude. From then on, the sessions got shorter.

Ben: I am suspended in space with my arms spread out inside a box. The box is transparent with non-transparent edges. I look like a light blue and transparent man. I see others in boxes around me.

Anat: Move back in time to the moment before you arrived at the box and tell me how that happened.

B: (pausing) I can't.

A: So, move forward in time to the moment you are no longer in the box.

B: I'm on Earth, on the ground. I'm a man with dark skin and straight black hair. I'm in my twenties. I'm not wearing anything.

A: Are you alone or are there other people around you?

B: There are people, but I'm alone. The people look similar to me. I see grass, trees, earth. Nothing special. I'm looking for something on the ground. Perhaps food, perhaps rocks... I find things that look like squirrels. I kill them and try to eat them. I feel alone. I'm trying to survive. I see other people trying to survive.

A: Move forward in time to a significant event in that same life.

B: I find a woman and kidnap her. I'm forcing her to come with me to my cave. I try to give her food and she refuses.

A: How do you feel?

B: I don't feel anything. I simply do what needs to be done. I'm trying to give her food and she doesn't want it, so I'm not trying anymore. I see that she wants to escape, but I don't let her.

A: Are you talking?

B: No. We're using signs.

A: Move forward in time to the next significant event and tell me what happens.

B: A child is born. The woman and I have a child, a boy. I feel happy. The woman is cleaning the cave. We lay the baby on leaves. I'm looking at the baby. I'm trying to imagine what he would look like when he grows up.

A: Move forward to the next significant event in that life.

B: The child is about twelve years old. The woman died. We are burying her outside in the ground and covering the grave with dirt and leaves. Both of us are sad because she died.

A: Move forward in time to the next significant event.

B: The child died. He was about twenty years old. I'm very sad that he died. I'm burying the child next to the woman. I'm crying. I'm sitting and thinking what to do, whether to find a new woman or not. I decide not to because she will die anyway, then the child will die, if there is a child.

A: Move forward in time to the next significant event.

B: I'm alone in the cave. I'm going to die as well. I'm very sad that I'm going to die. It is sad to die when I have no one. I'm afraid to die because I don't know what happens after death, but I'm also glad because I'm alone.

A: Move forward in time to the moment right after death, when you're no longer in your body.

B: After death, I am a white light watching my body. I'm happy to leave that body. I decide I don't want a life like that, being alone. I want a different life. I don't want to be alone in the next life. This is what's important to me.

Then I'm moving in space as white light. I have to decide whether to find other lives or return to the box. I decide to find another life. I'm flying in space towards a planet. I'm moving quickly towards Earth and merging with it, so that I would be born as life.

A: What happens after you merge?

B: I find that I am a king. I'm about fifty-sixty years old. I'm wearing a red and white robe and a crown. I'm standing on the terrace, looking at the kingdom. I'm very proud that I have a kingdom.

A: Move forward in time to a significant event in that life as a king.

B: Two farmers come to me for judgment. They stole something, so I have to decide on a punishment. They are to be slaves; working for the person they tried to steal from, for a month. I feel good because I gave a just punishment.

A: Move forward in time to the next significant event in that life.

B: We were conquered. I am no longer a king. I'm in a dungeon, chained. There are other people in chains. I don't know who they are. I don't recognize them. Everyone is dirty, humiliated, and looking down at the ground. I'm angry and frightened. I don't know what's going to happen.

A: Move forward in time to the next significant event.

B: I'm being released from that place because we were rescued. My kingdom somehow managed to defeat the conquerors. They saved me, and I'm a king again. I feel good that I'm a king instead of a slave imprisoned in a dungeon. I finally understand what it's like to suffer because before I was in the dungeon, I didn't.

A: What do you think about that? Did it change things for you?

B: I decide to release everyone from prison. After I release all the prisoners, people cease doing bad things. They don't steal anymore. Even though people know they won't have to be imprisoned if they steal, they don't. I feel good that my decision caused everything to be better. People feel better and there is no crime.

A: So what do you do as a king?

B: I decide how to divide the food among all, and who is right in all sorts of disputes.

A: Move forward in time to the next significant event in that life.

B: They bring me someone who has stolen something. Suddenly, someone stole anyway. They brought him to be judged. I don't know whether to punish him or not. I decide to punish him. The punishment is to be a slave for a month. Then people start stealing again, so I give more punishments and send some of them to prison. Everything returns to the way it was before.

A: How do you feel?

B: Not good. I thought I discovered how to make people not steal, but I was wrong. Or I don't know if I was wrong; it worked for a while and then it stopped. I don't know what to do. Which way to go?

A: Move forward in time to the next significant event in that life.

B: I am now an old man and I can't be a king anymore. They make my son a king. My son decides to release everyone from prison, like I did. For a while people don't steal, and there is no crime. But then they go back to committing crimes, so people are sent to prison again and made into slaves. I'm watching it happen, and I don't know how to guide my son.

A: Move forward in time to the last day of that life.

B: I'm going to die. My son is with me along with a few other younger sons, and they all respect me. I'm a little afraid to die because I don't know what's going to happen. I don't know if how I acted in that life was good. I feel that I tried to do good things. I feel some kind of acceptance.

A: Move forward in time to your final moments before you leave that life.

B: I feel that I shouldn't have sent people to prison in any case. I feel guilty.

A: Move forward in time to the moment after the transition, after you leave your body.

B: I'm a white light again.

A: What do you think about the life you have just experienced?

B: I think it was a good life. I saw that it was possible to go against what seemed rational and still have things get better.

A: What happens now, after you leave that life?

B: I am a white light, and I go back to the colorful planet. I simply merge with the planet. Then I become a being on the planet. I think I didn't spend enough time on Earth as a king. I want to return to Earth as a thief. I disconnect from the planet and return to Earth as a thief. I'm in a market trying to steal bread. They catch me and bring me before the King. He sends me to prison for a month.

A: How do you feel?

B: Not good. I don't like being in prison. I decide that I don't want to steal anymore.

A: Move forward in time until after you are out of prison. What happens then?

B: I want to steal again. I decide to be more careful so that I won't get caught. So I steal and get caught. Again, they bring me before the king to be judged. He doesn't send me to prison. He tells me I have every right to do whatever I want. If I want to steal, I will. I'm very surprised. I don't understand why I wasn't sent to prison or received punishment for stealing. I go back to the market and find that I no longer want to steal. I'm trying to think why I don't want to steal anymore if I won't face prison, because it's supposed to be the other way around. I'm trying to understand, but I'm not successful. Why don't I want to steal?

I'm still trying to understand, and I think that, maybe, it's because I feel free. I'm free to be who I am, so I don't have to prove anything, and I can do whatever I want. Stealing suddenly seems meaningless, considering all the other options I have.

A: What do you do next?

B: I become a merchant in the market. One day, I discover someone trying to steal from me. I decide to catch him and send him to the king so that he would be set free, and would not want to be a thief anymore, like me. I call the police, or the guards, to take him. They take him and I don't hear from him again. I feel good because I may have inspired him to give up thieving, like me.

A: Move forward in time to the next significant event in that life.

B: I'm going to die. I'm alone. I feel good, free. I'm a little afraid to die, but I feel good about my life. I'm not a thief.

A: Move forward in time until after you leave your body.

B: I go back to the colorful planet. I understand that on Earth there are things that work contrary to common sense, things that are not apparent until later.

A: *How did you reach that conclusion?*

B: I thought that if stealing was permitted, people would steal more, but the opposite happened.

A: *What do you decide to do now?*

B: I remain on the colorful planet and exchange information with other entities. I notice that more and more entities want to go to Earth. I'm pleased I caused other entities to test the things I said. After the information exchange with other entities, I leave the planet in order to find new things. I'm flying in space. I decide to be a star. I'm merging with a yellow star.

A: *How do you feel?*

B: Like a star.

A: *How does a star feel?*

B: Not exactly feels... it's a continuous movement inside itself, as if the body is in constant motion and heat. It feels like stinging. All the molecules are in continuous motion.

A: *Do you have any thoughts?*

B: No thoughts. There's only a feeling of movement all the time.

A: *Move forward in time until you leave the star and tell me what happens.*

B: I simply become white light again and go back to the colorful planet. I exchange information with other entities.

A: *Move forward in time to the moment you decide to leave the colorful planet.*

B: I fly to Earth. I become a storm. It feels good. I can destroy everything. I ruin and destroy. I know they will have to rebuild. I feel good that they have to start from the beginning. I destroy all evil and everything must be rebuilt. After the storm passes, I become clouds, watching from above. I feel good, now that they have to rebuild.

A: *Do you see what's happening down below?*

B: Yes. People are scared, looking for things, and they don't know what to do. I know it's temporary, and that everything will be fine in the end. It's good because the suffering is temporary. Things will be better than they were before.

A: *What's happening now?*

B: People are rebuilding.

A: *What's happening with you?*

B: I become white light, and I go back to the colorful planet.

A: *Then move forward to the next time you decide to leave the colorful planet.*

B: I'm exhausted...

A: *May I speak with Ben's subconscious?*

Subconscious: Yes.

A: *Why did you choose to begin where he was in a box?*

SC: To show him that everything is energy and thought, like he saw in the movie "The Matrix."

A: *You showed him a life in an early period on Earth. He lived in a cave with a woman and child. What was the purpose of showing him that life?*

SC: To show him that being alone and losing people are only temporary, so he shouldn't be afraid of that.

A: *He experienced life as a king. What was the purpose of showing him that?*

SC: I let him be a king to show that sometimes he can do things contrary to logic, and they still work. His brain is limited to conclusions and logic. Sometimes there's a need to go in a different or strange direction in order to achieve goals. When he was a king, it was only one side of the story. He didn't understand why his decision achieved a specific goal, so I allowed him the experience of being on the other side, that of the thief, to better understand why he stopped stealing. As a king, he couldn't understand it.

A: *Is there anything else you can add to why he stopped stealing?*

SC: He stated the reason. He felt free so he didn't have to steal. Freedom lifts the limitation of who he can be. He didn't have to be a thief. Freedom to steal allowed him not to steal.

A: After a while, although there was no punishment, people started stealing again. Why did they go back to stealing?

SC: They felt that the freedom not to steal somehow restricted them. They looked at themselves and saw that they weren't stealing, so they wanted to test the boundaries.

A: Then you showed him that he merged with a yellow star. What was the purpose of that?

SC: To show him what happens when you're not an entity with will, emotions, or curiosity. It was simply to show him what it's like to be something else.

A: What can he learn from that?

SC: To respect everything. Everything is an entity in itself. Everything has awareness. He shouldn't take things for granted. It's obvious that living things have awareness, but things that are not living do also.

A: Does everything have awareness, even objects?

SC: Yes.

A: He came back to Earth as a storm. Why?

SC: To show him that on Earth, even when bad things happen, it's for a specific reason. There are bad things that lead to good things. I let him be a storm, so he can see things differently, from the outside. He was the one that caused bad things to happen, but eventually they turned into good things.

A: Ben has a few questions. He feels insecure and anxious when he has to speak in public. Is there anything you can say about that?

SC: Ben has a problem being in front of an audience although lately less so. He thinks that everyone is watching him, examining him and judging him. Ben has to understand, by himself, that it's not true. If it happens, it's because he judges others and watches them. As soon as he stops judging, he won't feel judged, and he'll allow himself to be freer in front of an audience.

A: He has another issue with self-confidence. He wants to feel surer of himself.

SC: It's the same thing really. Ben feels unsure of himself because he thinks that others observe him, just as he observes others and places them into categories. As long as there are people who are inferior to him, in his eyes, there will be people who are superior to him. He should understand that both those he deems inferior and those he deems superior are actually like him. Then he will realize that his place in the world is equal to everyone's, and his confidence will increase.

A: There is another question that might also be related to that. He asks why he cares so much what other people think. Why does he need the approval of other people?

SC: Because he thinks that he's not good enough. He feels that whatever he does is to please others. He does things to please others because he feels that others are superior to him, and that he has no place in the world. Since he deems some people inferior to him, he feels that they have no place in the world. He perceives that there are always people who are superior to him, so he will always feel that he has no place in the world. He has to understand that everyone is the same.

A: He asks why he feels anxious when he is late.

SC: He feels nervous and anxious because this is how his parents behave. He needs to learn that he has his own opinions, and he doesn't have to behave the way his parents do. As soon as he understands that he is his own person and that he has a place in the world, this behavior pattern will evaporate. He will have his own pattern of behavior.

A: He asks why he has these parents.

SC: So he can understand that he is unique. As soon as he understands that he does not have to behave like his parents, he will feel great satisfaction, and his self-confidence will increase. This is one way to raise his self-confidence.

A: He asks why he doesn't have children yet.

SC: Because he is still a child who thinks that he should act like his parents. As soon as he understands that he does not have to behave like them, he'll be able to create a new and unique life.

A: Is there a way to help him get out of that pattern? Can you help him or make suggestions?

SC: He has to understand that his parents are their own beings with their own goals. Not all his goals are similar to theirs. To understand that, he has to know himself and what motivates him.

A: How can he do that better?

SC: He can listen to himself and silence the outside world through meditation.

A: How often should he meditate?

SC: At least three times a week.

A: What does that mean? Just to close his eyes and then what?

SC: In the beginning, he should close his eyes and not listen to anything. He should just observe his thoughts. Then, he can ask himself questions and wait for an answer until I reply.

A: He asks why he is depressed in the mornings.

SC: Because he doesn't feel connected to himself or his actions. He knows that everything he does during the day is not what he actually wants to do. It's not what he came to Earth for. Most days when he wakes up, all that burden of what to do, and the knowledge that he is not fulfilling his purpose weigh heavily on him.

A: Can you tell him what he is supposed to do? What he came to Earth for?

SC: No. He has to understand by himself.

A: Then meditating will help him with that?

SC: Yes.

A: Is there a preferable time of day to meditate?

SC: It is not important.

A: When I asked Ben if he believes in past lives and everything we are doing now, he said that he is still unsure whether it is real or not. Can you say anything about it to help him?

SC: No. Not at this stage.

A: Do you have any last message for him before we finish?

SC: No.

A: Thank you...

COMMENTARY

This session started with Ben suspended in a box. That showed him that all is energy and thought. Then he proceeded to experience different lives and existences, including other forms of awareness, in order to understand that everything has consciousness, including objects. It might be difficult to imagine what it would be like to be an object without will, emotions or curiosity. Perhaps we think that these attributes define us, and that there could be no consciousness without them. But it seems that consciousness is broader and more robust than we realize as human beings. For something to exist at all, some type of awareness may be required.

MESSAGES

1. Everything is energy and thoughts.
2. Do not fear loss and aloneness because they are temporary.
3. Sometimes logic is a limitation. Your thoughts may need to go in different and strange directions in order to achieve certain goals.
4. Everything has consciousness and needs to be respected.
5. Everyone is equally important.

STUDY QUESTIONS

1. How does the fear of loss or being alone affect your life?
2. How much do you allow yourself to think 'outside the box' and try new directions?
3. Can you think of bad things that happened in your life that later on led to good things?
4. Do you judge other people to be either inferior or superior to you?

AFFIRMATIONS

1. I overcome temporary feelings of loss and loneliness with the power of my eternal soul.
2. Because I keep an open mind, brilliant creative ideas easily come to me.
3. I choose to learn from everything that happens in my life, so I am constantly growing and improving.
4. Because I know that everyone is equally worthy, I am more and more confident every day.

SESSION FOUR

Flowing with Many Waters

THIS session was conducted during my visit to Israel. Ben wanted to ask about his girlfriend; he couldn't decide whether he should marry her or break up with her. He wanted a family, but wasn't sure she was the right person for him.

He also mentioned that he'd been thinking about the question of whether or not there was a finite number of lives or experiences on Earth. He gave the example of a photograph made of pixels. Within a set size or frame, there is a limited number of combinations or pictures that the pixels are able to form. This number could be very large, but still finite. He wanted to know if the number of experiences on Earth was limited in a similar way.

Ben: I see large rocks. Everything is kind of dry. There is a hole in the ground, like a tunnel.

Anat: Look at yourself. What do you look like?

B: I look like water. I feel that I must go into the tunnel. I have to enter the tunnel because I have no existence without the tunnel. I am becoming a stream inside the tunnel. I'm flowing.

A: How does it feel?

B: It feels right. I feel I'm doing what I'm supposed to. I'm flowing in the tunnel, and I'm not the only one. There are a lot of other waters flowing with me. I'm a part of the water, but it consists of many waters, like me. We're not exactly separate because we are connected. I know I'm moving ahead and see one angle, but apparently there are other points of view that are not mine. They're all parts of me like an entity with many heads.

A: Can you connect to the other points of view?

B: No. I'm only moving forward, slowly. There is no communication between us. Everything is silent and flowing.

A: *Do you know where you're going?*

B: No. I can see only a meter or two ahead.

A: *How do you feel about not knowing where you're going?*

B: I don't care. It doesn't matter because no matter where I end up, I'll still be water, and I'll go on. I'll get to where I'm supposed to go.

A: *Go to another time, another place...*

B: I'm a ship. I'm the ship of the Vikings; the Viking that I was before.

A: *Are you the ship itself?*

B: Yes. I'm sailing in rough water. There are many people walking on me.

A: *How do you feel about it?*

B: Good. I'm a ship because I'm supposed to be a ship. I'm supposed to sail, and I'm doing what I'm supposed to be doing, so it is good. I feel big.

A: *Go to another time, another place...*

B: I'm on a planet climbing rocks. I'm similar to a human, but a little bigger. I'm a light beige color. I'm wearing minimal clothing. I feel good. We are hunting, several others and I. We climb the rocks and dig because they contain large worms that we eat.

A: *What's your relationship with the other people?*

B: We're all equal. There's not much talk between us. We dig in the rocks and look for worms.

A: *Go to another time, another place...*

B: Now I'm a small whale, a female whale. I'm swimming with my calf. She's swimming with me, and sharks are chasing us. I'm very afraid. I'm thinking: *Just don't eat my calf.* We are swimming very fast, and the communication between us is a type of sonar, so I'm transmitting to her to swim faster and faster. But in my heart I know there's no hope; at some point they're going to catch us. Then the sharks get the calf. I feel awful; I couldn't protect her. They are eating the calf. I'm thrashing about in the water, but it doesn't help because more sharks are coming. Then, I see that the calf is already dead, so I escape. I swim far away. I feel alone... alone... I don't know what to do because there's no one and nothing around. I decide to commit suicide. I dive deep, as deep as possible, so that the pressure will crush me. I dive very, very deep until everything hurts... Then, I dive even deeper. Then it's all over.

A: *Move forward in time until you're no longer in your body.*

B: After I die, I go to the colorful planet again; then, I'm reborn on the planet. I tell other entities on the planet about being a whale and being helpless, and ending life because of helplessness.

A: *How do you feel about it now that you're on the colorful planet?*

B: I understand myself as a whale; why I committed suicide.

A: *What do other beings think about it?*

B: Other beings also understand because many of them had similar experiences. They chose not to continue their experience. It's a way of stating that I had enough. It's okay because there will always be more experiences. If I want, I can go through these experiences again.

A: *Do you have any desire to go through this experience again?*

B: No. I have no need because helplessness is the worst thing there is. It's like having no control over what happens. So this isn't something I want to experience, even if I know I can stop it by ending that existence.

A: *Move forward to another time when you leave the colorful planet to experience something different. Tell me what you decide.*

B: I've already decided. Immediately after the experience as the whale, I wanted to be the shark. I find myself again in the water, and I'm chasing after outcast whales. They're outcast because if they weren't, it would be much more difficult to chase them. There would be more whales to protect each other. Either they are lost or outcast. They're in very small groups that can be controlled.

A: *How do you feel?*

B: I feel like I don't want to kill, but I must in order to eat and survive. I'm chasing a small whale and her daughter. There are several sharks chasing them. There's still a feeling of helplessness, that I have no choice. I have to kill them and eat them. We're faster than the whales, so we catch the calf and slowly bite into her.

A: How do you feel?

B: I don't feel good about it, but I do it. It's not bad enough to stop. The hunger is too great. If I don't do it, I'll die. It's them or me. I can eat other small fish, but that means a lot of fish. It's better to eat a large whale, to kill one thing, than to kill a lot of small things.

A: Move forward in time to the end of your life as a shark.

B: I'm old, an outcast, because I can't contribute anything. I can only harm the pack, so they banished me. I need to make it on my own in the sea. I eat small fish, and I know that one day I will be eaten. I accept it because it's clear that it's the cycle of life. One day someone eats me, another day they will be eaten. I'm part of the natural food chain. I'm a little sad I'm going to die, but I don't feel bad about it. I know I'm part of the sea.

A: What happens after the shark dies?

B: I'm reborn on the colorful planet. Again, I share my experience with others. I speak with all kinds of entities who have experienced similar things. One felt helpless… Another felt helpless because he was imprisoned in his own need to kill or to eat. We try to think if it's better to be the whale or the shark. We conclude that it's better to be the shark.

A: Then what happens?

B: We are moving again on the planet and trying to choose where to go next. I decide to be a sun.

A: What is that like?

B: Flowing and noisy. Shaky. In motion all the time, but feeling as though I'm moving and not moving at the same time. Like a person standing in place and shaking very hard. It's a little like being in prison because I must be here all the time. If I weren't, there would be no life on other planets.

A: How do you feel about it?

B: I feel like a sucker. I'm not doing anything except being a sun and giving energy to other things. I'm not getting anything out of it.

A: *Go to another time, another place...*

B: I'm on a road, driving. I look like a car.

A: *How do you feel?*

B: Like a car.

A: *How does a car feel?*

B: Like a rock. Something like that, like something motionless. By myself, I can't move.

A: *How do you feel about it?*

B: A little restless. I can't move. I can only drive, only move quickly from one place to another. Within myself, I can't move...

A: *Go to another time, another place...*

B: I'm on Earth, performing in a magic show. I'm a magician. I'm facing the audience and doing tricks. Everyone is pleased, and they're applauding me. I feel good that they're applauding and pleased with me. They like me.

A: *Is the magic show all tricks?*

B: Yes. I'm asking for a volunteer to come to the stage for a disappearing act. A woman volunteers and gets up on the stage. I put her inside a box. I close the box, and then when I open it, she has disappeared from the box. Everyone applauds. I close the box again and then open it, but she doesn't reappear. She should have appeared, but she didn't. I ask my assistants, "What's going on? Where is the woman?" They say that they don't know. She was supposed to enter the box and then pass through a small tunnel to a small box next to it. She was supposed to pass through, but she never did. She just disappeared. I get anxious. Everybody is anxious, the audience is also anxious. She simply disappeared. She can't be found. The police come, then the ambulances come. The entire auditorium, inside and out, is being searched. They're taking apart the chairs. People are screaming, and her family is screaming. It's a mess, and I don't know what to do with myself because I'm responsible for the show. I'm responsible for the people, and I don't understand where she disappeared to. She simply disappeared. We can't find her.

Her family is suing me. I am a very successful magician, so I hire the best lawyers in the world. They prove, in court, that there was no malicious intent, and we didn't know how she disappeared. It was unintentional...

I'm declared innocent, but my entire career is ruined. I stopped doing shows, and I can't understand what happened. Where did that woman go? Everyone knew me because I was a very famous magician. If you're famous and something bad happens to you, everyone knows about it. I can't find another job, and the money slowly disappears. I don't know what to do with myself. I don't know how to live with myself. Something happened that was probably my fault because I didn't think about all the problems that could occur, of all the scenarios. I blamed myself, all those years... The woman's family believed, in the end, that I had done nothing malicious. They didn't understand how this could have happened and wanted me to tell them what could've happened and how. The curiosity killed us all and we simply had no answer. I have nothing to live for anymore, so I decide to commit suicide. Then I hang myself.

A: *Move forward in time, just after you die as a magician.*

B: After I die, I go back to the colorful planet. It's the first time I arrive at the planet with questions. How can it be that something impossible happened? Such things don't happen. There are always reasons. I ask all kinds of entities; I tell them about my experiences and say that I don't understand what happened to me. I ask others about what happened to me. I'm looking for answers, and I can't find any. Nobody knows. Then, I decide that it can't be. Somebody must know. Surely the woman herself must know. Maybe I'll find her here. I continue roaming the planet and encounter entities and ask if they know of anyone who experienced something similar. She was a regular woman who volunteered for a magic show and disappeared in a box. I can't find anyone who knows. That's it.

A: *So it was never resolved?*

B: I tell myself that it can't be. It can't be unresolved because everything has a cause. Everything happens for a reason. There are no questions without answers. I just need to find the answer. So, I decide to continue searching and won't stop until I find the answer.

A: And?

B: That's it. To be continued...

A: May I speak with Ben's subconscious?

Subconscious: Yes.

A: Why did you choose to show him that he was water flowing inside a tunnel?

SC: So he would better understand what it means to flow. To understand what it means to move in the right direction without seeing too far ahead... what it's like to know when you're progressing without seeing a final destination and knowing that it will be all right, no matter what.

A: Is this how he's supposed to live his life as a human?

SC: Yes. Instead, he constantly worries about what's going to happen. What will happen if what he expects to happen doesn't happen? He forgets that everything that happens is supposed to happen. In terms of the big picture, it doesn't matter if little choices lead him here or there. In the end, life is life, and one way isn't better than another. You just move on.

A: Are there some decisions, maybe bigger decisions, where it does make a difference what you choose?

SC: Ultimately, it's not that important.

A: After that, you showed him that he was a Viking ship. Why was that important?

SC: Because he was on that ship when he himself was a Viking commander. So he was shown the point of view of being a ship. He saw what it was like to be something bigger than what he was before, which was a Viking. He had to know about true responsibility. As the ship, he was responsible for all the lives on it. He had to know what it's like to not fall apart in the sea and have many lives depend on him, even if these beings were "bad" Vikings. He was still responsible for them, and it didn't matter if they were bad or not. He had to do his job and make sure they stayed alive.

A: How is that relevant to his life now?

SC: He should treat everyone with compassion and respect and not judge people. Sometimes, he simply has to take care of people, even if he doesn't like their behavior.

A: You showed him a life on another planet, where he climbed large rocks, hunted large worms and ate them. Why did you show him that?

SC: Because Ben is afraid of cockroaches. The ground produces all kinds of creatures that he finds repulsive. There are situations where this is reversed. The worms were not repulsive, and he even ate them. It's so he can see that things are relative.

A: You showed him that he was a mother whale, and the sharks in the water ate her calf. What was the purpose of that?

SC: Ben is afraid that if he has children, he won't be able to protect them because Earth is a cruel planet. I showed him that he is right. He won't always be able to protect his children, but the cycle of life is bigger than him. There's nothing he can do about it. He should have children even if he can't protect them. Just like the sharks eat, they get eaten in the end. It is all one cycle of life.

A: Is that a major reason for Ben not to have children?

SC: It's not a major reason, but that concern is there. Even if there comes a time when he can't protect his children, everything is temporary. And everything repeats itself.

A: Later you showed him that he decided to be a sun and felt like a sucker. Why?

SC: To make him realize that he has more power than he thinks he does. He doesn't know it, but he has the power to influence and the power to give energy to others. He doesn't do enough of that. He feels like a sucker sometimes, as if he wastes the energy he gives.

A: You showed him that he was a car driving fast on the road, but within himself he wasn't moving. What's the purpose of that?

SC: Ben likes to drive fast and...

A: That's also why he got a speeding ticket...

SC: That's why he got a ticket (laughing)... I wanted to show him that he's not alone on the road. There is also the car, and when he goes fast, he's part of the car. He goes faster to feel that he's in motion. But when he is a car that only drives fast and is not in motion, that is in fact what actually happens. Going faster doesn't mean that there's actual movement. You simply get from one place to another faster. It is only a matter of time, not movement. Ben has to find other ways to be in motion, not artificial ways.

A: *So he needs to have more motion in his life?*

SC: Yes.

A: *Then there was that experience with the magician and the woman who disappeared. What's the idea behind that?*

SC: Ben had an experience on Earth that he couldn't explain, so he should continue to search because there is an explanation. He shouldn't think that everything is easy to understand or ultimately has a simple explanation. He should dig deeper until he understands what happened there. That explanation is related to the nature of the colorful planet and to other types of entities that Ben hasn't met in the past, and that he should meet.

A: *Did the woman disappear in a way that is impossible to explain physically?*

SC: It can be explained, but Ben has to meet other entities to explain it to him, so that he can understand. Entities travel from planet to planet and see only one perspective from their entire experience. There are other entities, in different stages of their evolution, that see things differently, and they have to explain what happened to Ben.

A: *Are the entities he has to meet on Earth?*

SC: He should meet them on the colorful planet. On Earth, all the entities look the same, so he doesn't know how to recognize entities that are "different."

A: *But do they exist on Earth?*

SC: They exist, but he can't identify them, so he can't ask them anything.

A: *Will he be able to identify them on the colorful planet?*

SC: If he looks hard for them, he'll be able to.

A: *How is this story relevant to Ben's life now?*

SC: It's not relevant.

A: *So it's something for the future, when he returns to the colorful planet?*

SC: Yes.

A: Ben has a few questions. You recommended that he meditate, so he tried several times, but it was difficult. Can you say why it was difficult and maybe help him try again?

SC: It was difficult for him because he's still captivated by the world, by Earth, by all his thoughts, all the things that bother him. He needs to make more of an effort. There's no other way. After he forces himself to do it several times, it becomes easier.

A: So even if there are no results that are noticeable, he should persist?

SC: Right.

A: He also asks why it is difficult for him to take things lightly.

SC: Because he can't see what's going to happen in the intermediate future. The lack of knowledge about what will happen bothers him. Then he engages in all kinds of thoughts that cause heavy physical distress.

A: What do you mean by physical distress?

SC: Heart pounding and lack of sleep sometimes. A moderate physical distress, although the distress is completely disproportionate to the issue itself. There can be a lot of stress because of trivial issues as well as important ones. There is no correlation between the levels of stress and the severity of the issues.

A: How can he lessen the stress he feels?

SC: He should remember his experience as water and know that it doesn't matter where he flows. The flow is the goal, not the destination. There is always flow, and you simply take a detour sometimes; but that's all it is, a detour.

A: In a previous session he mentioned feelings of anxiety. You explained that it's because he had requested that interactions on Earth be accompanied by emotion. You said that you could change that feeling so that it wouldn't feel like anxiety. Ben says he still feels anxious. Can you help him with that?

SC: He should, again, practice meditation. Otherwise, it won't change. He needs to change his perspective. Sometimes he manages to do that, but he needs to practice much more, because he knows how to do it.

A: Why is it difficult for him to decide about his girlfriend?

SC: Because he lacks the knowledge about what's going to happen. It's difficult for him to see the unknown. Like the water that only saw a meter or two ahead, that's what he does now. Because it's difficult for him to see ahead, it's difficult for him to decide. He's not sure what kind of future he wants for himself.

A: Can you help him with that? Suggest anything?

SC: Again, he should be silent by himself and know that he might not reach any conclusions because they are transient and changing. He just needs to flow, and I don't know whether to call it making a decision or simply picking a direction.

A: Is there a direction that is preferable to another?

SC: I can't answer that yet.

A: This situation of indecision, is it all right to be in it?

SC: It could be all right, but not for Ben because he thinks about it and it bothers him. Because everything is, in fact, a flow, it doesn't matter that much. If there's a goal, then decisions have to be made. Ben feels that he has a goal, so it bothers him when he thinks he's not moving toward it.

A: Does he know what that goal is?

SC: His goal currently is to have a family with children.

A: Is that a good goal?

SC: Yes, for him.

A: So the problem with indecision is that he's not progressing towards the goal he set for himself?

SC: Yes.

A: Why is it difficult for him to take risks?

SC: It's related to his experience as water. He still doesn't understand that everything flows, and it's all the same, and it's all okay. He's afraid of the unknown. To him, it's risky to venture into the unknown, when he can't tell what his emotional state will be like afterwards. He doesn't know if he's going to be glad, sad, or afraid. Every risk opens up endless possibilities for bad things to happen. Ben doesn't want to feel fear, so he prefers not to take a risk and wants to stay safe. When he begins to flow, it won't look like a risk. While we are in an experience, we see things differently than when we look at it from the outside, with lack of knowledge. So we always manage. All this business of risks is actually one big illusion because we don't know what the next day would bring anyway. All our minor decisions also carry some type of risk, and major decisions are not riskier than minor ones. That's what has to be understood here. It's all an illusion.

A: So Ben tends to think of the negative things that can happen?

SC: Ben is aware of the positive things that can happen if he takes risks, but he prefers to postpone these good things because risk involves an option for bad things. So he holds back and doesn't take a risk.

A: Why is it difficult for Ben to believe that all of this is real, including the planet and all the other lives?

SC: Because he's captivated by the experience of Ben himself and of humans.

A: Would it be beneficial for him to believe that it is real?

SC: Yes. He should open his mind more and understand that the truth he sees in front of his eyes is also magical. There is magic in the physical, too. The fact that he is alive is miraculous. He needs to understand that the physicality he sees before him is no more reasonable than anything else in the world. If he tries to get to the colorful planet in his imagination, it will help him believe more.

A: Why is the experience here on Earth so captivating that it's difficult to see beyond?

SC: Because if people on Earth could see beyond, they wouldn't be experiencing Earth. They'd be experiencing something else. They'd experience the colorful planet more than Earth because they'd know that it's a temporary experience. If they knew that it was a temporary experience, they'd have no challenges. They would have no obstacles to overcome.

A: So it's intentionally hard here?

SC: Yes. Intentionally. Even someone who meditates and connects to his essence will never reach that place completely. Even if he believes in it, he won't experience it totally. If he did, he would immediately die and return to the colorful planet.

A: Why does Ben feel like he's making up the stories in the sessions?

SC: Because his brain doesn't allow him to do otherwise. He can't experience them because he's not there. He is here on Earth, so he must make them up or feel like he's making them up.

A: *Does he only feel like he's making them up?*

SC: Yes. The experiences are real, but Ben doesn't feel it because of a limitation of the human brain.

A: *Ben spoke of existence on Earth. He asks if it is finite and if it repeats itself. He gave the example of the picture where all the pixels are repeated.*

SC: Yes. Everything repeats itself. Every life repeats itself. There are many, many options for lives. There are more options than there are entities that want the experience. Entities can experience life again on Earth, or, as other people on Earth. But at some point, the entities finish their experiences on Earth, so there's no need to create more options. There are enough.

A: *So when an entity lives as a specific person, he can experience the same life again as himself, differently, with perhaps different choices?*

SC: Yes. He may if he wishes to do so.

A: *Can he experience the same life as say, his mother, or a friend and interact with himself?*

SC: He can live as whatever he wants because there's always room for any configuration he wants to experience in life. The role will not be taken by another entity. There will always be room. If it were taken, then he would still be able to have the experience, in a different session.

A: *For example, when Ben was a king and then a thief, was Ben both people at the same time? Was he a king and a thief and was there an interaction between them?*

SC: Both were not at the same time. Ben was both a king and a thief, but when they were interacting, it was another entity interacting with Ben.

A: *Then one entity cannot interact with itself in different roles at the same time?*

SC: No.

A: Can you tell Ben who is actually speaking now? Who am I talking to? Who is answering these questions for Ben?

SC: I am.

A: Who are you? Can you explain?

SC: I am Ben's Mediator.

A: What is a Mediator?

Mediator: Whenever an entity travels from the colorful planet to another one, not necessarily Earth, it has a Mediator. It has a link to the colorful planet. It's like a power cord, in your language, between the planet and its image or a part of the planet. In this case, it is to Earth. So I'm a part of the colorful planet that controls and watches Ben. I don't exactly control him, but I know what he's supposed to do. Sometimes I talk to him, and we decide together what needs to be done. I'm a part of the planet that remained... a part of Ben that stayed on the planet.

A: Does everyone have such a part?

M: Yes.

A: Does everyone come from the same colorful planet?

M: Yes.

A: Is it a physical place?

M: You can say it is physical. I don't know what physical means, but it exists.

A: Does it exist in our universe?

M: It exists in our universe. Yes.

A: Is there more than one universe?

M: Yes.

A: An infinite number of universes?

M: There is an infinite number of universes, but these universes are interactive with each other. That is to say, if there's an interaction between people, it can... Let's just say, you asked if Ben could talk to himself... Ben can't talk to himself at the same time, but can speak with himself in a parallel universe.

A: So there's another Ben there?

M: Yes. There's another Ben. Maybe even several Bens. How to describe in physical terms... let's say that there's a ball, with all kinds of marbles inside. Let's say it's two balls with marbles and they are parallel, in terms of time. So actually, in terms of time, this universe is parallel to another universe and there are interactions between the universes.

A: Do the different Bens live exactly the same lives, or do they make different choices?

M: They can make different choices. It's up to them.

A: You're saying that there's an interaction between them. So is it like considering options? Is it like looking at the future and seeing what happens if different choices are made?

M: It's not looking at the future. This simply happens all the time. If someone chooses something, and someone else looks at the same thing and chooses something slightly different, an interaction can occur between the two beings.

A: So is it true that whenever a choice is made, another universe is created that represents a different choice?

M: You can say that.

A: Then it's almost infinite?

M: Yes. It's a type of infinite.

A: Is Ben's Mediator in charge of all of them, or does every Ben have a different Mediator?

M: Ben's Mediator, who is I, is in charge of Ben... Yes. I am in charge of all the Bens. I'm in touch with all of them at the same time.

A: Do the interactions between the Bens go through you?

M: No, they don't. They go through the universe, not through me.

A: In addition to Ben, do you mediate other existences?

M: Yes. I operate all sorts of things.

A: All kinds of experiences in different places at the same time?

M: Yes. The time element is a little different than the earthly term, but yes.

A: Can you explain the concept of time? I understand that there is no such thing as time; it's only an illusion. So what is it actually?

M: Time is a construct. It's not something that is needed, in principle. It exists so that people can have watches... and so that they'd know what occurs before what, what causes what, what event happens, and what can cause something to happen. In fact, it's all an illusion. Everything happens all the time now.

A: So everything happens forever?

M: You can say that...

A: Does that mean that Ben's life never ends? Does it always exist?

M: It always exists, but it's not always there. In other words, it's always there like a container. It's not like Ben is always... For example, if Ben wants to be a king, he can return to being a king, and he can return to being exactly the very same king he was before. But it doesn't mean that he's a king, at this moment, all the time. The template is simply there. The template always exists.

A: Then the template of the life of Ben always exists?

M: Yes. If he wants to experience it, he can. If someone else, another entity, wants to experience Ben's life as Ben, he also can. He'll experience exactly what Ben experienced.

A: And make the same choices?

M: He will make the same choices, and in terms of time, as you say, it's like a journey back in time. But this is meaningless because everything happens the same way. Again, it's like going back in time, but it really doesn't matter.

A: So, if another entity can experience Ben's exact life, and all the decisions stay the same, it sounds like everything is predetermined and there is no free will.

M: He can experience Ben's life, but he can experience it a little differently than Ben. He can do whatever he wants.

A: So there is a template of his life. Can it be modified?

M: Yes. If someone wants to experience the emotions Ben experienced, he can. If he wants to experience the same choices Ben made, he can. If he wants to experience a change in choices Ben made, he can change these choices.

A: Does that mean that in another time I can be Ben and Ben can be me?

M: Yes.

A: And life would be the same, only my entity is inside Ben and vice versa?

M: Yes, if we choose to; if Ben and Anat decide to do so.

A: What would be the purpose of that? To experience the other side?

M: Yes, because when the entities separate from the planet... in fact, all the entities are parts of the planet. When they are born and leave the planet, they have a will of their own and an independent need to experience things. Then, you can say that because everyone is of the same planet, part of each entity experienced something from another entity. But if the entity wants to really know, he should himself experience the lives of others, too.

A: Is there only one colorful planet, or are there more?

M: I can't answer at the moment.

A: You said that all people on Earth come from the same colorful planet. Does that mean they are all connected?

M: Yes, and they all exchange information.

A: What's the purpose of gathering information on the colorful planet?

M: To create intrigue, so that other entities will want to experience things. That's generally the purpose.

COMMENTARY

From the perspective of water, there is no destination, only flow. Water has no control over its own flow; it flows according to the laws of physics and gravity. It follows the path of least resistance. Would it serve us as humans to live in a similar state of mind and have a similar attitude? A lot has been said in different spiritual teachings about living in present time. What if we could just 'be in the flow' and trust that everything would be all right? If every life is just one of many, then we might as well enjoy every moment and not worry about the future. If happiness comes from within then what's really important is how we feel about ourselves — not the circumstances we find ourselves in.

The experiences as a whale and a shark demonstrate the cycle of life. Both beings experienced suffering and limitations. But the suffering was temporary. It was only in the context of those lives and was chosen as an experience to go through. Death and loss are parts of the experiences here on Earth and have to be accepted. All experiences are temporary and come to an end.

As a magician, Ben had an experience that he was not able to understand. Even when he got back to the colorful planet he could not find an explanation for the experience. It seems that there are still mysteries even beyond the existence on Earth.

MESSAGES

1. The journey is the destination.
2. Treat everyone with compassion and respect.
3. Accept the cycle of life, which includes death and loss.

STUDY QUESTIONS

1. How can you tell when you are moving in the right direction without seeing ahead too much?
2. Are you in the habit of worrying about the future?
3. Do you give to others regardless of personal gain?
4. How often do you turn down opportunities because of fear?

AFFIRMATIONS

1. I accept the grace of this moment, knowing that I am in the right place doing the right thing.
2. I am safe and secure because I trust in the flow of life.
3. The more I give to others, the more fulfilled I feel.
4. I am excited about the different opportunities life presents me with.

SESSION FIVE

A Pharaoh in Disguise

THIS was the first of a few sessions we conducted online using Skype because I returned to the USA, and we wanted to continue. It worked pretty well, but it was a bit stressful not being face to face. We never knew if we could get through the session without technological glitches. We considered having him stay in the U.S. to have more sessions in person.

Ben: I see dirt. Black dirt. I am a man, wearing a black jacket. I'm walking with other people who are wearing black jackets. I'm thirty to forty years old. I feel anxious because I have to take care of all those people.

Anat: Are you responsible for them?

B: Yes. We're walking in an area that looks like it has been bombed. Everyone's looking for food and trying to survive. We're walking together as a group of about twenty. We arrive at a building and go in. There's food there. Another group of people is eating the food. We ask for food, but they don't want to give us any. So we start a war. We have sticks, and we beat them up. We win. We have many wounded, but at least we have food. We throw the other group out of the building into the street. We eat the food.

A: How do you feel about what's happening?

B: I don't have a problem with this. We all need to eat and survive. There's no choice.

A: Move forward in that life to the next significant event.

B: I'm sitting on a chair and in front of me there's a person on the gallows. He's about to be beheaded. Someone asks me if we should proceed, and I tell him to go ahead. The person is executed.

A: How do you feel?

B: I feel okay. Apparently, this man was trying to steal food from us and got caught. We kill people who steal food from us.

A: *What happens next?*

B: We keep searching for food and continue walking down the road through the ruins. There is chaos. People keep to themselves, and we do too. As a group, we're able to survive better than others who are alone.

A: *Are there women in the group?*

B: Yes.

A: *Children?*

B: No.

A: *What does it look like around there?*

B: Looks like after a nuclear holocaust. Everything is black and gray, and there are ashes in the air. The sky and the clouds are gray. People are looking for somewhere to go and wondering how to survive. Looking for food. It is very hard, and there is no hope.

A: *Move forward in time to the next significant event in the same life.*

B: We're surrounded by a group of people larger than ours. They want to take our food and all our belongings, but we're not letting them. We are defending ourselves, but they outnumber us. They are at least fifty people and we are only thirty. We can see that they have the advantage, but we know that if they take things from us, we're going to die anyway, so we have nothing to lose. They come at us with sticks, and we fight for our lives. Since they outnumber us, they win and take all our food. They kill some of us, so there are about twenty left in our group; twenty people with no food or anything. We don't know what to do and we're wounded. There's nothing to eat, nowhere to get food and things for basic needs. So we continue searching, and we see larger groups that have come together. We realize we don't have a chance unless we join a larger group. We're looking for larger groups of people to join, but none of them will let us because that would mean less food for them. On the other hand, if we join, the whole group will be stronger; but they don't agree and reject us. We go on and eat scraps from the floor in some of the ruined buildings. We find all sorts of small things we can eat, but it's hard... very hard. Somehow, we manage to collect some food, but again, a larger group arrives and kills us. We simply disappear. We die.

A: *Tell me what happens in the moment just before you die.*

B: That moment is chaotic because we're being beaten on our heads, legs, chests, and faces. All that in order to take our food. We have no strength to defend ourselves anymore; then, everything becomes dark and we die.

I leave my body. I'm quite shocked by the experience. I wanted to understand what it would be like to be responsible for others. I realized that if I only take care of those in my closest circle, there's no chance of survival.

A: *Do you decide anything about your next life?*

B: I decide that in the next life, I'll take care of everyone and not just my closest circle.

A: *What happens next?*

B: I return to the colorful planet. I'm reborn there. I share what I experienced and what I saw. I want to understand how that situation turned out that way. Why was everything in ruins like it was in a war?

A: *Don't you know why it was like that?*

B: No, I don't.

A: *What do you find out?*

B: I feel that I was born... somehow it had always been like that... the planet... It's as if it was always in ruins. I don't remember myself living there as a child. So I ask the other entities about the story behind that place. They tell me that planet is unlike most places you go, where you're born, you live and then you die. Simply, whoever wants to get there from the colorful planet just arrives there and has an experience that lasts for about half a year. He's not born there. He becomes an adult immediately and has only that experience without anything before.

A: *What do you think about that experience when you're on the colorful planet?*

B: I'm glad it was only for a short time because it was terrible. It caused me great suffering to be there. I'm glad I didn't have to live there for years and years.

A: *What do you decide to do next while you're on the colorful planet?*

B: I decide to roam around and communicate with other entities in order to find more places to visit.

A: *Move forward in time to the moment you decide on a place.*

B: I simply die inside the planet to be born in a new place. Then, I find myself on Earth, as a Pharaoh in Egypt. I'm very rich and powerful.

A: *How do you feel?*

B: I feel powerful. I feel omnipotent.

A: *Move forward to a significant event in that life.*

B: I find myself in a marketplace with many people there. No one knows I'm the Pharaoh because I'm dressed like everyone else. I'm in disguise. I want to hear what people think of me, and what people on the street say about me. So I walk around the market and start up small talk with people: what's going on with the Pharaoh? What do people think of him? I see that people are afraid to speak. They are very, very afraid. I ask why they are so afraid, and they reply, "What? Don't you know? Whoever speaks unfavorably is executed. You have to show respect for the great Pharaoh. If you don't show respect, you're punished." I see that no one really likes the Pharaoh and only fears him. When I return to the palace, to the kingship, I don't understand why people are scared. Actually, I do understand that. What I don't understand is why they don't like me. After all, I'm doing everything right. I'm the great Pharaoh and if people don't respect me, they deserve to die. I don't understand why that's a problem and why people don't accept that. I decide to pick random people from the marketplace and hang them in the town center, to show everyone that if people don't like me, they have to be hanged. I execute them in front of everyone. Then everyone applauds me and likes me.

A: *So everyone likes you?*

B: Everyone shows they like me, so I'm very pleased.

A: So you feel good about this?

B: Yes. I really want people to like me, so I decide to kill more and more people because the more people I kill, the more people are afraid and the more they like me. I slowly annihilate the majority of the population, and my advisors and family are the only ones that remain. Then I realize that there's almost no one left to like me. I still don't understand why or how I got into a situation where the majority of the population is gone, and I don't feel loved.

A: How do you feel?

B: I feel alone.

A: Move forward in time to the next significant event in that life.

B: I'm going to die. I'm already very old. After I realized that it's impossible to force people to love me, the population increased slightly because I stopped killing people. I feel that people no longer want me to be king. People are less afraid of me because I stopped killing. I stopped punishing. I don't care because I'm going to die anyway, so I just accept it. I accept that I killed for nothing, and apparently that's why I deserve to die too. I accept death as punishment.

A: Do you decide anything about your next life?

B: I decide that I won't force anyone to love me and that no one can be controlled that way.

A: May I speak with Ben's Mediator?

Mediator: Yes.

A: Why did you choose to show Ben the planet in ruins, where he had to survive with a group of people?

M: Because Ben forgets that he is a part of everyone, a part of one essence, one universe, and one consciousness. He took care of the people around him and took from others. He separated himself from the "community" and took care only of himself and his closest circle. I wanted to show him that there's really no separation. Everyone is the same one. Everyone is the same and all take care of each other. Just as Ben himself consists of many small parts, he is also a part of one big machine.

A: *How does he have to live his current life according to this understanding?*

M: He should look past his circle, look at people less fortunate who need help, and try to help and understand them. He needs to realize that he is a part of them and they are a part of him. He shouldn't separate himself from them, just like others shouldn't separate themselves from him.

A: *Why did you choose to show him a life as a Pharaoh, when he was killing people to make them like him?*

M: Because he thinks he can make people like him sometimes. He thinks he has to make people love and respect him. He should understand that it's impossible to force these things to happen. Everything has to come from within. Everything has to come from the positive and not the negative. He thinks that if he makes people feel sorry for him, they'll love him and want to be with him. But people will love him for himself, for his positive behavior.

A: *What positive behavior for example?*

M: Being in a better mood because he can be a kind and funny person when he's in good spirits. Sometimes, he chooses to be sad and withdrawn because he thinks that it will make people want to be closer to him, but it causes the opposite. It makes people not want to be around him. So, he should operate out of positivity and not negativity.

A: *Ben asks why he doesn't renovate his apartment.*

M: He thinks that if he renovates the apartment, it means he'll stay in that apartment and stay in that life. He's afraid of staying in that life.

A: *As if renovating the apartment is an acceptance of the situation he is in now?*

M: Yes. But it doesn't mean he'll remain in it. It doesn't mean he won't change, and it doesn't mean he won't move forward. This is just another thing he would do, to live better at the time. It doesn't mean anything about the future, or where he'll be or what he'll do.

A: *About the future, he asks whether he should remain in his job or quit now.*

M: Ben should probably leave that job. He's very comfortable at work, but he fails to appreciate his job and feels that he needs a change. Besides finding the change within himself, he needs to make some kind of external change. That can help him.

A: He also says that sometimes he postpones and avoids these sessions. He would like to know why.

M: Because he knows that he doesn't like to make changes. He knows that the answers are not always easy for him to hear, so he prefers not to hear them.

A: In one of the first sessions we had, we talked about Ben's fear of change and you explained the reason for it. You said that it was because he was afraid to die on the colorful planet and that you could reduce the fear of change. Is it reduced now?

M: No, not yet. He still takes things too hard and not as sort of a game. He needs to connect to himself more. Otherwise, he'll continue to fear changes and take reality too hard and not as it really is, a segment in a journey.

A: When you say connect to himself, do you mean meditation again?

M: Yes. Meditation and more meaningful thoughts about himself.

A: He also asks why he doesn't trust himself to get the answers in the sessions.

M: Because he has no experience with finding answers for himself. He relies on other people to give him answers and tell him what to do about the major decisions in his life. He doesn't see himself making decisions that are good for him. The way to do this is to simply make decisions and see what happens.

A: These were Ben's questions. I wanted to ask: the information you are giving us is very interesting and important. Why is it all right now that this information will reach people? That they will know that the colorful planet exists and that this life is only one segment?

M: Because many people are less busy with survival and are busier with unimportant things, and they want things for themselves. It's important that they know there's something beyond their own lives. People are not kind to each other. They think they are individuals, just as Ben thought on the planet I showed him. If people knew that they are part of one thing, a very positive thing overall, they would see things differently and there would be less suffering. Then, the entities from the planet would no longer need the experience of suffering in order to appreciate the positive in their lives.

A: So, experiences of suffering exist so that entities will appreciate the good?

M: Yes, and to understand what suffering is because it's a part of the range of emotions and reception abilities of entities. Entities can experience an infinite number of emotions and intensities, so these are simply two sides of the same coin. There's no good without bad and vice versa. However, it is possible to appreciate the good with less suffering.

A: Is this the reason why this information is available now, so that people will understand that we are One?

M: Yes. Because people on Earth have already developed technology, and their resources are directed more towards destruction and less for survival. There's more curiosity about destruction. What happens if they harm another person? How will they feel?

A: So you're saying that this information is important, so that people will change their attitude and life will be better here on Earth?

M: Exactly.

A: Do Mediators have Mediators, too?

M: Yes.

A: Is it infinite? Are there always more and more Mediators?

M: It is more circular than infinite.

A: So at the end it repeats itself?

M: Yes.

A: How is the concept of soul, or spirit, related to the concept of the colorful planet? Is there such a thing as a soul?

M: Yes. There is a soul. The soul is the essence that dies on the colorful planet and is reborn on Earth. It is the colorful essence that also returns upon death to the colorful planet.

A: When a person is on the colorful planet, does he have a Mediator there as well?

M: Yes.

A: *So is the Mediator a part of the colorful planet or from another place?*

M: He is a part of the colorful planet.

A: *Are there Mediators in other places, not on the colorful planet?*

M: Yes.

A: *Is there a concept for God? Is there such a thing as God?*

M: There is such a thing but not in the sense that is believed on Earth.

A: *So in what sense?*

M: In the colorful sense of the word. In fact, the Mediator of the colorful planet.

A: *Does he have a Mediator too?*

M: Ultimately he has a Mediator, in a sort of a circular way. The one who mediates that God is another type of God in a chain that eventually repeats itself.

A: *Then actually everything is one entity?*

M: Everything is like a brain of a human being with thoughts. Then God, you can say, is the thought, and the entities on the planet are more like the atoms of the brain. Something like that...

A: *If everything is thought, does this mean that everything actually exists, that there is no such thing as fiction?*

M: Yes. Everything exists because everything is actually thought.

A: *So, if an entity wants to experience life of, say...*

M: She can experience anything.

A: *If she wants to experience what it's like to be Superman, even though it's a fictional character, can she experience it?*

M: Yes.

A: *So everything actually exists. Is there such a thing as fiction?*

M: No.

COMMENTARY

In this session Ben described a situation in which he was completely focused on survival. He was competing with other people on resources in order to survive. Killing other people did not solve the problem. Everyone died eventually and there were no winners.

Here on Earth people forget or don't accept that we are all connected. We identify with different types of tribal groups, based on country, religion or even skin color. But we are all the same, and life can be much better here if we remember that we are all parts of one thing, one consciousness.

In his experience as a Pharaoh, he tried to use force in order to make people love him. He learned it is not possible to make that happen by using force.

MESSAGES

1. There is no real separation. We're all One.
2. There is something good beyond our human lives that we are part of.
3. It is impossible to get love and respect by force. Everything has to come from within.

STUDY QUESTIONS

1. On what grounds do you separate yourself from other people?
2. Do you try to get people to love or respect you by using force?
3. What type of positive behavior may help you connect better with people?

AFFIRMATIONS

1. I am connected to All that exists; therefore I always see the beauty of life around me.
2. People love and respect me because I express love and respect for them and for myself.
3. My positive attitude enables me to live up to my full potential.

SESSION SIX

It's Too Bad I'm a Tree

THIS was the second session we conducted on Skype. Ben said he was feeling unhappy at that point in his life. He had choices to make about his home, career, and love life, but he wasn't making them. He said he was afraid to let go of things that were familiar. He also had concerns about leaving Israel for an extended period of time and coming to the U.S. to work on the book; he was afraid of feeling uprooted.

Ben: I see grass and trees. I look like a tree. I feel stuck. It's too bad I'm a tree.

Anat: Why?

B: Because it's impossible to move. Besides moving branches and leaves a little, I can't do anything.

A: What would you like to do?

B: Maybe travel a little. There are other trees, but there is no communication with anyone. It's somewhat convenient that there's no need to talk, but it's a little boring.

A: Do you have any sense of time? How long have you been there?

B: I have no sense of the time. It seems like forever.

A: So leave that for now and go to a different time and place.

B: I'm still a tree. There are people who want to cut off my branches.

A: How do you feel about that?

B: Not good at all. I can't escape. They want to cut off my branches and leaves in order to make firewood. I'm shaking my branches, but it's not helping. They're cutting off my branches.

A: How do you feel?

B: Helpless. I'm an old tree and it's unlikely I can grow new branches.

A: *Move forward in time to the end of your existence as a tree and tell me what's happening.*

B: At the end of this existence, I'm completely without leaves. I'm very dry and still stuck in the same place. I want this experience to be over already.

A: *Move forward in time until you're no longer a tree.*

B: I'm flying through space in the dark. There are many stars around. I'm simply flying. It's not clear to me what I am, but I have some awareness. I don't have a body or anything. I fly and then merge with a planet, like a Moon, without light, without anything. A gray planet. I become a gray planet.

A: *How does it feel?*

B: Heavy and useless. It's some type of a planet like a moon. It has nothing on it; it's like a huge rock. I'm stuck again, just like when I was a tree.

A: *Move forward in time until you're no longer that planet and tell me what happens.*

B: I'm on Earth. I am a chunk of gold. I'm stuck in the ground. I also feel stuck, but people are looking for me. They want to dig and find gold, find me because I'm very valuable. I feel I'm being exploited. I don't feel worth anything. But because there aren't many like me, for some reason I'm wanted.

A: *Move forward in time until something happens.*

B: I'm found by some people who are digging in the ground, and they're beating me with a hammer. On the one hand, I'm pleased that I was found, so that I can leave where I am. On the other hand, I feel very used. People don't care about me, only my price.

A: *What happens next?*

B: They take me out of the ground and divide me into pieces, and I'm all the pieces together.

A: *How does it feel?*

B: It doesn't feel like I'm in pieces. I feel as if I'm aware of everything that happens, all the places where I am. I am broken into six pieces. I'm aware of all of them. I don't feel divided, but I know I am. I'm sold to all sorts of different people, and I'm transferred from one hand to another.

A: *How do you feel about that?*

B: Exploited. Used. It's not clear to me why they do it. There's nothing valuable in me. I have no contribution beyond existing.

A: *Are you aware of what's happening with all of the pieces?*

B: Yes. They simply transfer me from hand to hand. I find myself in rings, too, with silver and gold. I'm worth a lot. People get a lot for me. They give a lot for me, things that have value. I mock whoever uses me that way because they don't really know what's important and what's not. They want me so that they can give me away. It's as if people don't understand what true worth is. They think I'm worth a lot because other people want me, and other people want me because they think that other people want me, so it's a circle that has no end. It seems strange to me that people value me so much.

A: *Move forward in time until something happens, or until you are not gold anymore.*

B: I'm moving in space again. I'm flying, and I see a spacecraft, a spaceship from Earth. I choose to be the man inside the ship. I'm inside the spaceship. I have to conduct all sorts of experiments and I'm alone.

A: *How do you feel about being alone?*

B: Lonely. I would rather have other people with me, but the mission is to be alone.

A: *How do you feel about the mission?*

B: I feel good because I chose to do it. I chose to participate in the mission.

A: *What exactly are you doing there?*

B: I'm experimenting with all kinds of gases. I have to inhale them to see if I can breathe in space. I have all sorts of gas tanks with different densities. I'm trying to breathe to find out how it feels. We want to develop another way to breathe in space, a more efficient way.

A: *More efficient than oxygen?*

B: Yes, and easier, a way that would make it easier to carry to space. To carry oxygen is relatively complex. So I breathe all sorts of different compounds of gases. Some get me high, some don't. Some make me feel sick, some don't. That's all I'm doing actually.

A: *How long are you supposed to be there?*

B: Approximately a year.

A: *How's this year going? How do you feel?*

B: The year passes with a lot of sleep because there is a special gas they gave me to sleep. So I sleep through many days because then the effects of the gas on my body are monitored while I'm sleeping. I don't have to be awake for much of the time, so the days go by quickly. I can sleep continuously for a few days. I feel relieved because I didn't agree to a normal year. I agreed to a fast year. So it's not that bad.

A: *Move forward in time until something happens.*

B: The day that I'm supposed to return to Earth arrives. I activate all the instruments and begin to fly back to Earth. I feel good that I'm finally going to see my wife and kids. I feel pretty excited. I fly back to Earth and land safely. There's a very nice reception. My wife and kids come. We're all very happy that I got back home. But it's difficult for me to remember them.

A: *What do you mean?*

B: I have all sorts of memory lapses. I don't remember names sometimes. I'm having tests done, and they say that it's because of all the gases I tested. Some have side effects they didn't know about. They say they hope the side effects will eventually go away. They don't; they only get worse. The memory lapses are getting longer. This worries me. Then, somehow, they become manageable. They still occur every once in a while, but I live with them. I have no choice. I take all kinds of pills for memory improvement. I manage to live a relatively normal life.

A: *How do you feel?*

B: I feel bad. I regret going into space because I'm not in a good condition. Because of memory problems, things are difficult for me. It's quite difficult for me to do things, remember places, remember faces and names. Sometimes I don't remember my family. It's embarrassing at times. I'm quite remorseful about going to space.

A: *Move forward in time until after you're dead. Tell me what you think of that life, now that you're no longer in the body.*

B: I don't like the life I've just lived because I felt not in control without my memory.

A: *Are you making any decisions about your next life?*

B: I decide that I won't do anything that will cause me to lose my memory or lose control.

<hr>

A: *May I speak with Ben's Mediator?*

Mediator: Yes.

A: *Why did you choose to show him that he was a tree and felt stuck?*

M: So that he would know that when he is stuck, he is not protected. He thinks that if he feels stuck, it means he's protected. He has a home, a job, and things he can hold on to. To show him that it's an illusion, that feeling stuck doesn't mean nothing's going to happen. If he's not stuck, he has more control; he can control things that happen to him. It's better not to feel stuck.

A: *We were talking about the idea that Ben will take some time off and come here to have more sessions together. Ben said that he's afraid of feeling uprooted.*

M: There's no such thing as being uprooted; there are only thoughts in the brain. Feeling uprooted means that he's not aware of what thoughts he'll have in the future. When he knows what his thoughts will be, it provides an illusion of protection, or of not being uprooted, but this is only an illusion.

A: *Later you showed him that he merged with a planet like a moon. He was a gray planet and felt heavy and useless. Why did you show him that?*

M: That's a continuation of what I showed him before; the same reason I showed him his experience as a tree. A heavy gray planet in motion is actually worse than being a tree because he can't move anything. It simply exists and serves no purpose. It doesn't give or receive anything. To show Ben that now he is in a much better situation than when he was a gray planet. Ben sometimes feels like the planet, like he doesn't contribute anything. I wanted to show him that it is never true. He always contributes something and receives something even if it's not apparent. He should know that he's not like that planet.

A: *You showed him that he was a chunk of gold on Earth. What was the purpose of that?*

M: To make him realize what people like him actually think of certain things. They credit things with importance beyond what they really have. Gold is precious to everyone, but its value is an illusion. Many things that Ben considers to be important are actually not that significant. I wanted to show him that people behave according to what they *perceive* as important. So that he would know to distinguish between what is important and what is not.

A: *Can you give examples of things that Ben thinks are important but actually aren't?*

M: Ben thinks the way other people perceive him is important. It may be important to Ben, but not as important as he thinks.

A: *So what is really important?*

M: What type of a person you are and to what extent you make others feel good about themselves. It's something Ben doesn't always do. He thinks that by making others feel worse about themselves, he himself will feel good. Actually, it's quite the opposite. By making others feel good, he will feel better himself.

A: *Is there any significance to the fact that he felt used as gold?*

M: He felt used because nobody asked him what he wanted. Did he want to be dug out? Did he want to be taken? When he was gold, nobody asked him what he really wanted. Just like now, as a man, no one asks him what he wants. However, if asked, Ben doesn't know what he wants. He feels that on the one hand, he has free will to do what he wants, but on the other hand, he has to conform to society and to his parents' wishes. He vacillates between freedom and his wish to please others.

A: *What can he do about that?*

M: It's very difficult to become free of the desire to please. Ben should give more weight to what he wants rather than try to please others.

A: *How can he know better what he wants?*

M: He has to listen to himself more. He should practice meditation. Otherwise he only thinks he knows what he wants, but in reality he does not.

A: *He said it's very difficult for him to meditate because he has no patience for himself.*

M: He must make an effort. I can't help him with that. I can't show him the light or give him any insight about the matter. He must make an effort. There are no shortcuts.

A: *You showed him he was an astronaut in a spacecraft conducting experiments. Why?*

M: To show him that he could feel like an important man doing important things and have a very large ego. But that doesn't guarantee anything about the future. When he lost his memory, his self-importance did not benefit him because he couldn't remember much. Many things are transitory and it's impossible to know what the future will bring. Ego and achievements are not that important. All is temporary and there are no guarantees. Everything can change.

A: *What is important then?*

M: Making other people feel good and feeling good about oneself. Ben should know how to recognize these important things. He shouldn't try to please or impress other people, nor should he do things just to feel important.

A: *Ben has a few questions. He asks why we are stuck with the same personality throughout our lives.*

M: There's no point in changing one's personality before life is over. One can just die and get reborn. But sometimes we have parallel personalities.

A: *What do you mean by parallel personalities?*

M: The same soul can be several parallel personalities at the same time. So the Mediator is working with several personalities at the same time.

A: *In the same life? In the same body?*

M: Not in the same body; in different bodies.

A: *Are you referring to different incarnations, or parallel universes?*

M: In the same universe, several entities in parallel.

A: Do you mean different incarnations?

M: You can call them incarnations, but they all exist at the same time.

A: But not in the same body?

M: Not in the same body.

A: As another human being, for example?

M: Yes.

A: Let's say there's Ben, and at the same time, there is someone else in Russia, for example, who has a different name and lives at the same time? Something like that?

M: Yes.

A: So how are they related to each other?

M: They are related through the Mediator.

A: Do they affect one another?

M: Yes.

A: Can they meet?

M: No. They can't. But if they meditate, they can get signals from each other through the Mediator. If one entity reaches a conclusion, the other entity is able to more easily reach the same conclusion.

A: So they can learn from each other's experiences?

M: Yes.

A: Ben is not married and has no children, so he doesn't feel "normal". He asks why this is so.

M: Ben doesn't feel "normal" because he has more decisions to make, and he can't allow himself to reach decisions half-heartedly. Many people make decisions half-heartedly, but Ben wants to make decisions in a more educated way. He has processes to go through until he becomes "normal."

A: Is there progress with these processes?

M: There is a little progress.

A: What can he do to advance this progress?

M: He needs to believe and trust in himself more.

A: Regarding these sessions, he said that he does not trust his own answers. Can you say anything about that?

M: He really doesn't trust himself because he has no experience with trusting himself. He should simply accumulate experience.

A: *We talked about him coming here, to the United States, to work on the book. Do you think it's a good idea?*

M: It can be a good idea. It can contribute to his spiritual development, and yours.

A: *So would you recommend doing this, even though he's afraid of leaving his job and making a change?*

M: I recommend it. Yes.

A: *Can you say something to help him overcome his fears?*

M: It's going to be all right.

A: *Ben asks why people are afraid to be alone, without a partner.*

M: Because they are afraid that no one will be with them when they are disabled.

A: *Do you mean when they're old and unable to take care of themselves?*

M: Yes.

A: *Is that why people are afraid to be alone even when they're young?*

M: It's one of the reasons. People are afraid to know themselves well and know their limitations. If they are alone, they'll be "stuck with themselves" rather than busy with an interaction. They are scared of the experience of themselves.

A: *What can you say about that? Can you recommend anything?*

M: It's advisable not to be alone because people need interactions. Humans are made to interact, but when they are together, they must leave room for their alone time. There must be two parts of life, alone and not alone, one in conjunction with the other.

A: *Are there times when it's beneficial to be alone?*

M: It can be useful if one takes advantage of that period. If one uses it to get to know oneself, then it can be beneficial.

A: *How can being alone be used to get to know one's self?*

M: By looking inward.

A: *Meditation for instance?*

M: Yes.

A: *Why is it difficult for people to be happy?*

M: Because they don't combine the two elements of togetherness and aloneness. Humans need interaction, so they interact and don't make time for themselves, or they are alone, preoccupied with thoughts of themselves. So the two must be combined.

A: Why is it difficult to be in a relationship?

M: Because each partner sees that balance differently. No one is really balanced on the two elements of being alone and together. Usually one partner wants to be more alone and less together, and the other wants more together, less alone. They are opposites, so there can be no balance.

A: Is there a solution to that?

M: The solution is for partners to discuss these issues and clarify what needs to be done, but people don't do it. Each one thinks he knows what he needs, but this can never be exactly what the other needs. A few have made this work.

A: So a compromise is needed?

M: Yes, and people don't like to compromise. People think they're always right.

A: So everyone thinks that their way is correct?

M: Yes.

A: But that's not true?

M: No. Each one is a little bit right.

COMMENTARY

This session was about illusions. Being in a familiar situation provides the illusion of safety but does not guarantee it. The tree was not safe even though it was stuck in the same place. In life, movement and flow provide greater control than being stuck.

The value of gold is also an illusion. Many things that we perceive as important are actually not so. We need to recognize what really is important. Ego and personal achievements are not important because they are temporary.

MESSAGES

1. Staying fixed in one situation or condition does not guarantee being in control.
2. People always contribute and receive even when it's not apparent.
3. What's really important is to what extent you make others feel good about themselves.

STUDY QUESTIONS

1. Are there situations where you allow yourself to remain stuck because it feels safer than change?
2. Do you have a clear idea of what is really important in your life?
3. Are you generous with others and help them feel good about themselves? How do *you* feel when that happens?
4. To what extent does the need for approval affect your decisions and your life?

AFFIRMATIONS

1. I have confidence in my own judgment, so I move forward easily when the time is right.
2. The kinder I am to other people the better I feel about myself.
3. I live my life with honesty and integrity, therefore I approve of myself.
4. Because I approve of myself, I have no need for approval from others.

SESSION SEVEN

Born to Grow Rice

THIS was another session on Skype, with Ben still hesitant to leave his job or make any other changes. He did, however, ask for some time off from work. He also complained that he couldn't find enough interests in life and wanted guidance about that.

Ben: I am a merchant in a market. I'm carrying a bag with a lot of candles inside. I'm shouting, "Candles! Candles!" People aren't buying them. Sometimes they do, but it's not enough to take care of my family. I'm thinking about closing the business because there aren't enough customers. People don't want candles. My wife and I are arguing about closing the business. She asks me what I'm going to do if I stop selling candles. I tell her I don't know; maybe I'll try to sell something else. My father used to sell candles, so it was passed from father to son. The whole family sells candles. We argue, but I wouldn't close the business.

It seems that if things don't improve within a week or two, we will fight again. So I try to sell candles in the market one more time. With the exception of a few buyers a day, people don't buy them. A week passes, and again, we argue about closing the business. I'm slowly becoming convinced to close it. The question is what I would do if I don't sell candles. We discuss what I can do, what I can sell. We both decide to sell bread. People always need food. We start baking bread; we sell it, and it works better. After a few years, it stops doing well because there are many others selling bread. We don't know what to do and I'm out of work for a few weeks. I decide to look for work in designing houses and buildings because I have a talent for it. I become self-employed and have my own office for the design and drawing of buildings. I make a lot of money.

Anat: How do you feel about that?

B: I'm doing something that I love. I feel good.

A: What happens next?

B: That's it. That's how I live my life.

A: So move forward in time to the last day in that life and tell me what happens.

B: On the last day, I'm very sick. I have a problem in my lungs because I smoked most of my life. It's very hard for me to breathe. Because work required me to sit and draw at a table, I drank too much coffee and smoked a lot of cigarettes. I regret that now.

A: How old are you?

B: Eighty.

A: Move forward in time until you leave your body and tell me what happens.

B: I'm some kind of energy in space between the stars.

A: How does it feel?

B: Kind of emotionless...

A: Any thoughts?

B: No. There's only a desire to find a new place and see new things.

A: Move forward in time until you find a new place.

B: I get to a planet that's all water and nothing else. The water is raging and storming. I'm just an observer. I don't understand why this place exists. There's only water and storms, and the planet is black and dark blue. I'm trying to figure out why this planet exists. In the end, I find myself back at the colorful planet, and I want to be born in the water planet to see what kind of experience I can have there. So, I simply die in the colorful planet, go through the whole process and find myself in the planet's core with noisy, turbulent water. I find myself filled with emotions. It's as if I'm actually the core of this planet, full of emotions that are changing all the time. All types of emotions, jealousy, love, hate... all the good and bad feelings... I feel them all at once and that's why this planet is raging because it's actually the expression of all these emotions. Since I don't know how to contain all that I feel, I make myself agitated and stormy. I make myself rage so that I can somehow contain it and release the energy of emotions. Because it's so rough and hard, and I can't relax, just constantly feel and think all the time with no rest, I decide to explode. I know that planets can explode, so I concentrate very hard, and I explode into an infinite number of pieces, so that I can stop the experience, which is something very, very hard to contain. Again, I find myself in space as awareness looking for a place to be.

A: *Move forward in time until you find something.*

B: I decide to return to the colorful planet and listen to other entities describe things worth experiencing and where I can be. I roam there and exchange information with all kinds of entities.

A: *What do you decide?*

B: I decide I want to be on Earth as a Chinese person. I'm born to a couple who grow rice. As a child, school is very difficult. I'm an only child with no brothers or sisters. Everything is very routine. Every day, I go to school, study eight hours a day and do several hours of homework. I'm allowed to play, but not wildly. Only catch, hide and seek, and board games with friends are allowed. It's very straightforward and conventional. I'm fine with it. As a teenager or an adult over the age of twenty, I think about what to do in life. Because my parents are rice farmers, we decide together that I should also grow rice. So I spend all day in the rice fields and feel good about it. I don't think much about whether I'm fulfilled or not. It's what my parents wanted, so that's what I do. I don't think about doing something else because I don't let myself think about it. Everything is so clear and so decisive.

One day, a fire burned down our entire rice field. It's our livelihood. We grew rice because that's all we knew how to do. Suddenly, it's gone. Because we don't know what to do, my father and I decide that we have to be servants of rich people. So we start working for such people, growing rice for them, cleaning their home... I realize that because all I know about is rice, I'm screwed. I have to work for other people, not for myself, not for my parents, just for other people. Others tell me what to do, and it's strange after many years of working alone and being self-employed. Suddenly we are employees and others tell us what to do. I realize that I shouldn't have worked with rice. I should have expanded my horizons to do other things.

A: *Move forward in time until the last day of this life and tell me what happens.*

B: In the end, we went back to working with rice again. We set up fields once again and took out loans to buy new rice fields. Now I have sons of my own who work with me, and I regret having directed them to work with rice, as I did. Although I knew it was not the best thing to do, I directed them to it. I deeply regret that. Then I die.

A: *What happens after you die, after you leave that life?*

B: I decide that I want to be a rock star, a singer. I find myself as a singer of a very successful rock band. When I'm on stage, everyone shouts and loves me. I'm filled with energy. I always wanted to know what it's like when everyone loves me in an endless way. I wanted to know how I would feel when it happens.

A: *How do you feel?*

B: While it's happening, I can't really feel it because whoever loves me doesn't know me. I see that people love me with no reason, only because I'm famous. We're very successful, so people project on me all sorts of things they like, and they don't even know me. When people love me in this way, it reduces their value in my eyes because I suddenly realize that they can't be very smart. Because I don't appreciate them, I don't appreciate their love for me, and it doesn't make me feel better. So I understand that it's all a great illusion. The realization that their endless love is meaningless causes a deep depression. Then, because I'm very depressed, I start taking drugs to be a little happier and a little more joyful. I'm happier during the time the drug is in my blood, but after it's gone, the depression comes back together with the disappointment with the love that's missing. I don't appreciate people who try to love me, moreover, I despise them. I don't care if I'm loved or not because I think that people can't truly love because they don't really know anything. I realize that love is a big illusion that has nothing to do with reality.

The only love is... The only real thing is what I feel for myself. Because I'm so disappointed with the entire world, I can't feel any love for myself. It's a hole I've fallen into and can't climb out of. So I take more and more drugs and nothing can heal that big hole inside of me. We continue to perform, and every time, people are shouting while I'm singing. I'm a little high when I sing and everyone loves me, but that's only because I had drugs and alcohol before the show. All the negative emotions are mixed with a little high, so everything is fine for the moment. After the show, I take more drugs to cure the depression, but they don't work. I decide to end my life because nothing is enough and nothing is fulfilling. So I leave that life. I take some sleeping pills, mix them with drugs and simply fall asleep and don't wake up.

A: May I speak with Ben's Mediator?
Mediator: Yes.
A: Why did you choose to show him that he was a merchant selling candles?
M: So that he knows he can do more than one thing in life. He thinks that because he's already doing something... He works on computers, for example, on a specific project... he thinks it's what he should do his entire life because it would be the simplest and the easiest to do. He insists on doing something familiar even though it no longer works for him. This is to show him that he can find other things to do. Even if it seems like he knows how to do what he does best, there are other things he could learn to do even better and succeed even more.
A: Do you have any suggestions for him? What other things, for example?
M: No. He should explore by himself.
A: Does that mean he should leave his job and look for something else?
M: Not necessarily. He can find something else at the same workplace. Do something else. It doesn't matter much how he does it.

A: You showed him a planet that was all water, and he decided to be born there. It was a place where he felt a lot of emotions. Why did you show him that?

M: I wanted him to see what happens when emotions are felt but can't be controlled. So everything rages with no purpose, and nothing can be contained. So he would realize that because he's not a planet, he's a man, he can control feelings of jealousy, hate, and love. He can try to control, rest, try to experience the emotion and see that even if he feels something in particular, it's fine. The emotions are not raging, and everything is not experienced all at once. Because he's a man, he doesn't feel it all at once. He feels one emotion at a time. When he feels one particular emotion, it feels like a storm of emotions to him, but it's not. It's one emotion that he can feel and learn from.

A: How can he learn from his emotions?

M: He can try to understand why he feels the way he does, and what causes a particular feeling. If he doesn't like a certain feeling, he can change its cause.

A: Can you give an example?

M: He feels jealous. He's jealous of people who have spouses and children, who "have it made". He thinks that he should also have a family. He is jealous of other people who fulfilled themselves that way.

A: What can he do about that?

M: He has two options: try to move in that direction, get married and have children; or accept himself as he is and focus on his positive traits. He should know that everyone has problems. What happens is sometimes hidden, and everything happens in its own time.

A: You showed him that he was a Chinese farmer who grew rice. He chose to grow rice because that's what his father did. Why did you show him that?

M: To make him realize that he doesn't always have to do what's expected of him. Even in this life, he usually does what is expected of him. It's very hard for him to let go of his parents' expectations. I wanted to show him that if he doesn't free himself from them, he's going to regret it and perhaps even do the same to his children. Everyone has his or her own path. It's important not to be subjected to the wishes of others and not impose his wishes on others. People should be allowed the freedom of choice, to decide for themselves what's best for them.

A: Then you showed him a life as a rock star, where he was very successful but depressed. Why did you show him that?

M: He always wanted to know how someone that gets so much love feels. How could that be and what would he do with so much love? I wanted to show him how it feels and that in fact, there's no such thing as love besides loving yourself. There's no such thing as love, really, that is true to the end and pure.

A: Is there no such thing with humans or in general?

M: With humans.

A: Don't people know how to love purely?

M: No.

A: Does Ben know how to love himself?

M: Yes. He doesn't do it enough, but he knows how to.

A: What's the way to do it? I'm sure many people will be interested in knowing how to have more self-love.

M: The moment people keep promises they make to themselves, they love themselves.

A: Is that all it takes? Keeping promises we make to ourselves?

M: Yes, as long as these promises transcend one's limitations. If a person keeps a promise even though it's difficult, he will feel self-love because he has crossed some kind of a boundary and he exists.

A: Is it a personal achievement?

M: It's a type of achievement, but it is more like proof for the existence of the person, his place in the world. People don't like themselves because they think they have no place in the world, so when they keep their promises despite difficulties, they feel their own existence and that's when they love themselves.

A: When you say promises, do you mean big things or small things, like exercising for example?

M: It could be anything that is difficult for the person to do, small or large. And if you do good things for others, it also opens the door for them to do things that will allow them to overcome their limitations and love themselves.

A: Can you give Ben a suggestion of a limitation that would be beneficial for him to overcome now?

M: He can try leaving his job and see what that does to him.

A: He told them that he wanted some time off. Are you saying that it's better to simply resign and see what happens?

M: I cannot answer that. It's very difficult for Ben to quit. He's very captivated by the illusion of the job. But if Ben wants to really grow, maybe he should resign.

A: Ben is thinking about coming here, but he said that he didn't know if this is the right time because he feels the need to move forward in terms of having a family. He thinks that if he comes here, he won't progress in that direction.

M: Ben has to decide what he wants, so that if he comes for a visit, it will not prevent him from progressing toward having a family.

A: Ben asks why he doesn't find any interest in life.

M: Because he thinks it would mean he has to change and change his existence. He's afraid of change.

A: So, is it the fear of change that prevents him from finding interest in life?

M: Yes, it is. And he is also not looking. In fact, there is an infinite number of things one can do in life. One just has to look, and Ben is not looking. The things he already knows about don't interest him. However, if he looks for new things, he will find many that might interest him.

A: So the solution is to start looking for new things in order to find interest?

A. Yes, and to take into account that change can be a good thing, and he doesn't have to be afraid of it.

A: Can you give him some ideas on how to start looking?

M: Read books.

A: What kind of books?

M: Any kind, just read.

A: How can people be happier in life? I know it's a challenge for many people, and they're unhappy.

M: Being happy has to do with self-love, and just overcoming small limitations will create joy.

A: Why don't people do that?

M: Because they are in equilibrium at all times, and they have a limitation to break through boundaries. Their thoughts are moving in a straight line, and breaking away from that line takes energy. They think if they break away, move their brainwaves towards other things, they will lose energy. That's not true. People don't lose energy from movement. Basically, no energy is wasted; it's only displaced.

A: So the straight line is actually unchanged. Does it mean that the next moment will be the same as the one before?

M: Not exactly... not in terms of a moment or occurrence, but in terms of brainwaves. The wave goes from the known to the known, one known moment to the next known one. It's the path of the least resistance. It's like water flowing the shortest way possible, in the shortest, most natural channel. It's the same with brainwaves. Because brainwaves move from one known moment to another, every occurrence in life appears to be similar to the one before, and so life becomes routine.

A: Do people need to change that in order to love themselves more and be happier?

M: Yes. They should change their brainwaves and invest that energy in change.

A: Are you saying that we have to change all the time, otherwise one routine will become another?

M: One needs to be careful because constant change can be a type of routine as well. One needs to change when it feels like a change is needed.

A: Is it possible to know when it's time for a change?

M: If you listen to yourself, you'll know.

A: Is Ben in a place where change is needed?

M: Yes, he feels that he's in a linear state.

COMMENTARY

Ben was shown a life as a merchant in a market. He had to change careers a couple of times and ended up being successful doing something that he loved to do.

Then he experienced being a water planet in order to see what happens when all emotions are felt and can't be controlled. As a man, he is able to understand his emotions and control them by changing the cause of the feeling.

As a Chinese person he worked in the family business, growing rice. He did what was expected of him and learned the consequences of that.

He was shown a life as a rock star because he wanted to know what it would be like to have so many people admire and love him. He learned that what's really important is how one feels about oneself.

MESSAGES

1. You can do more than one thing in life.
2. Emotions can be understood and controlled.
3. Everyone has to follow his or her own path.
4. Keeping promises to the self creates self-love.

STUDY QUESTIONS

1. Are you living up to your full potential in your current life choices?
2. Do you take the time to understand your feelings and their causes?
3. Do you trust that you know what's best for you better than other people? Do you trust others to know what's best for them?
4. Are you in the habit of keeping promises you make to yourself?

AFFIRMATIONS

1. I seek out opportunities to express my talents and creativity; therefore I feel fulfilled.

2. Because I am in touch with my inner wisdom, I follow my own path confidently.
3. I do my best to keep my promises; therefore I love and accept myself completely.

SESSION EIGHT

A Self-conscious Mouse

THE following session was also conducted on Skype. We were still discussing the idea of Ben coming to stay in the U.S. to have more sessions, but he remained hesitant about leaving Israel for an extended period.

Ben: I see trees and leaves. I don't have a body. I think I'm some kind of wind, wind that blows leaves. I try to push them where I want, but there are other winds that try to do the same. It's like a battle between the winds; who can push the leaves where they want. I feel some kind of resistance in many different directions. The leaf doesn't know where to go or where to blow because all the winds are trying different directions. I'm looking for more leaves to blow; and again, others try to blow them in different directions. I try to blow in the same direction as another wind. I feel resistance, so I try to fly with the wind that opposes me. Rather than resist it, I fly with it, and then the two of us are blowing the leaf together, each one pushing it a little in the same direction. The general direction is the same for both of us, and we fly much faster, the leaf flies much faster. It's much better to fly together.

Anat: Move forward in time until something important happens or until you're no longer wind.

B: I'm in a basement. I am a mouse.

A: What are you doing?

B: I'm hiding. There are cats in the house, and I'm hiding so they won't find me. I'm also looking for food. There's no food. There are only scraps of unidentifiable things and they're pretty disgusting, even for a mouse. I wait for nightfall so that I can get out of the basement and look for food.

A: *What happens at night?*

B: At night when everyone is asleep, I get out of the basement, walk around the house, go to the kitchen and manage to climb on the table using the chair. There's a piece of bread I begin to eat. I eat fast because I'm afraid someone will discover me. When I finish eating, I quickly head back to the basement and manage to get there. Everyone's asleep. That's it.

A: *Move forward in time to the last moments of life as this mouse.*

B: I'm trapped in a mousetrap. It's a painful trap, not one of those where you just enter a cage. I know the owners of the house will kill me. I'm terrified, and I know there's nothing I can do. They'll kill me because they don't care about me. Then they kill me.

A: *Move forward to the time after the mouse is dead and you're no longer in your body.*

B: I'm in a hot air balloon. I'm a guy in his forties. I seem to be flying over Scotland or something. I'm alone. It's quiet and calm, except when I light the fire. Besides that, it's very quiet and pastoral.

A: *Move forward in time until something happens.*

B: I'm not able to direct the balloon where I want, so I'm drifting with the wind. I release hot air out of the balloon to make it land. Somehow, I manage to land in a field, and I have no idea where I am. I take all the air out of the balloon and spread it on the ground. I pack it, fold it and put it in the basket. I see houses in the fields so I go to one. I knock on the door and nobody answers. I go to another house, and they feed me. They give me a place to sleep and call the rescue forces to come and get me. That's it. Then everything's fine.

<hr />

A: *May I speak with Ben's Mediator?*

Mediator: Yes.

A: *Why did you show Ben that he was wind trying to blow on a leaf?*

M: To make him understand that if going in a certain direction is difficult for him, he can go another way, and it'll be easier and better for him.

A: *Can you give an example from his life now of a direction he's trying to go in, but is difficult?*

M: He always struggles with what he wants to do, what he wants to be, and how he can get satisfaction out of life. He should know that he could take another direction, flow more and not think too much. He thinks too much about what others have, and he doesn't. He needs to think more about what he does have and flow with it. He has his health, a relationship and capabilities. It doesn't exactly mean he should accept everything, but he shouldn't be preoccupied with what to do with these things. He can flow with them. Even if he didn't have them, he shouldn't take it so hard.

A: *What was the purpose of showing him life as a mouse?*

M: To demonstrate to him that every thing in life is important and every thing has self-awareness in some way. He shouldn't take for granted that he's a man because he could be other things, "simpler and inferior." He should appreciate his life more and the fact that he is human. Sometimes he wonders what would happen if he were dead.

A: *You showed him he was in a hot air balloon and landed in an unfamiliar place, but at the end things worked out. What was the purpose of that?*

M: To show him that no matter what happens, he'll manage. It doesn't matter if he gets to an unknown place. At the end he'll find something to help him find his way back. He will manage anyway.

A: *Why is it important to understand that?*

M: Because he's afraid of not being able to manage. He's scared of the unknown, but he'll always find something that will work out for him.

COMMENTARY

As wind, Ben learned that if it's difficult to move in a certain direction, it might be time to choose a different direction that is easier and better.

He experienced being a mouse in order to better appreciate his life now as a human being. He has to appreciate the gift of life more.

When Ben was flying in a hot air balloon he landed in an unfamiliar place, but everything turned out okay in the end. He should not be afraid of the unknown.

MESSAGES

1. Struggle less, flow more.
2. Every thing is self-conscious in some way and is important.
3. Appreciate the gift of life.
4. Do not be afraid of the unknown.

STUDY QUESTIONS

1. When you feel like you're struggling, would you consider trying a new direction instead?
2. Do you remember to appreciate the good things in your life?
3. Do you allow fear of the unknown to affect your attitude and decisions?

AFFIRMATIONS

1. Because I choose to be in the flow of life, I reach my goals easily.
2. I am grateful for all the positive things in my life and glad to be alive.
3. I now know that life brings good things to me, so I feel safe and secure.

SESSION NINE

Slave and Master

E VENTUALLY, Ben came for a visit in the U.S. so that we could have more sessions in person. This is the first session we had after he arrived.

Ben: I'm in the sea. I see lots of jumping fish and I'm one of them. It is stressful. There isn't enough time because we're like sardines jumping in the water with bigger fish trying to eat us. I see a lot of sardines jumping out of the water. Each one is trying to escape by jumping out of the water and then back into the water while swimming. It's chaotic. There's no cooperation between us. We're in the same place, but it's a complete mess. We're not swimming in unison. We're jumping out of the water.

Anat: Move forward in time until something happens or until you are no longer a fish.

B: Now I'm running in a field. I'm a horse, a beige horse. I'm running in a field with other wild horses. There are no people around. We just run. I feel good. Free. We do not communicate except for an understanding that we have to look for food. We eat hay, grass.

A: Move forward in time until something happens or until you're no longer a horse.

B: I'm on Earth. I think I'm a black slave. I live with a white family. I also have my own family. We are slaves to the white family. We're very afraid of the whites. They're in control. They're better than us and we have to serve them.

A: What do you do? What is your job?

B: My wife cooks, and I take care of the horses in the stables. I have two sons who work in the field. All day long they work the land. We live in a shack that's barely enough for two people and we are four. We're given bread to eat and water to drink and some sugar, sometimes a little rice and very simple things. We have no freedom because we're slaves.

A: How do you feel about that? What thoughts do you have about having to serve them and that this is your life?

B: It's difficult for me to work hard, but it seems clear that this is how it should be.

A: Is that because there is no other option?

B: It's not that there aren't any other options. It's how things should be. They're more evolved and more intelligent. We're inferior. Just like dogs are not masters of people, but the other way around, that's the way it should be.

A: Do you accept this situation?

B: Yes. I feel good about the fact that nobody expects anything from us, but to work and live our small lives. My wife doesn't expect anything special from me either, because we have our roles and we fulfill them. That's all.

A: How do you feel about your children, your sons?

B: I want them to be strong so they can work the land well for the whites.

A: What is the shack like?

B: It's like a room with dividers in the middle. Not really rooms, partitions.

A: Is there a kitchen?

B: No.

A: Restroom?

B: No.

A: Where do you go to the bathroom?

B: There's an outhouse.

A: Does the white family have a restroom in the house?

B: They have several. They have a very large house with two floors.

A: How many people are in their family?

B: There's the man, the woman, and their three children. The man's parents live with them.

A: *What do they do? Do they work?*

B: They have a chain of hotels. They own hotels and manage them. More accurately, the man is the manager and the woman does nothing.

A: *So you run their household?*

B: Yes. Not all of it. My wife cooks, I take care of the horses, and my sons are in the field. There is another family of slaves. They do everything else.

A: *Are you in touch with the other family?*

B: Yes, but we don't have a good relationship. We're not their friends or anything. We don't have friends.

A: Do you work every day?

B: Yes, every day. On Sundays we work less, but we work most of the time.

A: *Do you have any education? Can you read or write?*

B: No.

A: *Move forward in time until a significant event happens in this life.*

B: We are being freed. There was a war between the South and the North. All of us are being freed.

A: *How does it feel?*

B: Strange, because we don't know what to do. We can go anywhere we want, but because we have no place to go to, we ask to stay in the shack. We ask the family to let us stay in the hut and in return we work for them. That means that nothing changes except now we work fewer hours, we can go to town and wander around more freely. There are other slaves... no longer slaves... There are many black people running around free in the city. This feels good.

A: *How do you feel about the white family now? Is there a difference?*

B: No. We are still afraid of them because we know that if we don't do a good job, they can kick us out.

A: *Move forward in time to the last day in this life.*

B: I'm lying in the hut. I'm very sick. I have pneumonia. I'm eighty years old. My wife and my children are there. Looks like I'm dying.

A: *Do you have any thoughts about death?*

B: No. I accept it.

A: *Let the transition happen and let your consciousness leave your body. Now you are hovering and looking down on it. What do you see?*

B: I see a pathetic man. That guy lived a life for nothing except to serve someone else. It seems pathetic to me. I decide I don't want to be in this situation again, serving someone else.

A: *What do you do now, after leaving this body?*

B: I decide that I want to be the one he served.

A: *So what happens?*

B: I become a white child in the family. They have slaves.

A: *Your slaves are the same family?*

B: No.

A: *Is it another family? Is it the same situation with different people?*

B: It doesn't matter if it's the same family because everyone's the same.

A: *So you're a child in the white family. How do you feel?*

B: I feel that everything is taken care of for me. I don't have to do any work. Our family has slaves. My parents are never angry with me because when father gets angry, he takes it out on the slaves. Mother too. So I have no problems.

A: *How old are you now?*

B: Thirteen.

A: *Move forward in time until an important event happens.*

B: I'm twenty. There's a war and all the slaves are freed. I'm crying because I won't have anyone to do things for me. I'm afraid I won't know how to manage without slaves and have to work. Some of the slaves remain because they have no place to live. They still do a lot of work, but all the relationships change. My parents yell at me because I need to do things and learn things. I don't understand why these slaves were freed. Why did the world become so bad if it could have been good? Why did they make it bad? There are slaves; and if there are slaves, why shouldn't they serve us? I don't understand this.

A: *What do your parents say about this?*

B: That some people think that slaves should live like ordinary people. My parents don't understand why, but they say that nothing can be done. This is what's happening. We need to deal with the new situation. I have to deal with this new situation.

A: *What do you think about the idea that slaves should live normal lives?*

B: I can see some justification for it, but not quite. I don't believe it. I don't feel it. I still think that if we're white, good and civilized, and they're black, they should serve us and thank us for giving them something to eat and a place to sleep. I'm very, very angry with everyone, with the whole world. I feel that everyone is against me and my family. They took from us something that is very, very precious.

A: *So what happens? What do you do?*

B: I decide to look for slaves or look for blacks on the street, who will come and stay with us and serve me. I offer them food and a place to sleep to just come and serve me. I slowly get used to the fact that they do most things, but not all.

A: *Move forward in time to a significant even in this life.*

B: One day, a few blacks break into the house and capture me. They hang me on a tree, as revenge for all the years we did those same things to them. We hung them and beat them.

A: *What thoughts go through your mind when they hang you?*

B: I'm very afraid. I don't have any coherent thoughts, just terrible fear.

A: *Allow the transition to happen and your awareness to leave your body. Now you are hovering above it. What do you see?*

B: I see a pathetic man who could do nothing for himself and had others do everything for him. I decide I don't want to be like that, to live as that kind of man again. I decide to be a good man, the kind that serves people out of respect, kindness and a real desire. If he's served, then it's for the same reasons. To be more balanced.

A: *May I speak with Ben's Mediator?*

Mediator: Yes.

A: Why did you choose to show him that he was a sardine in the sea?

M: So he would see what a real mess is, and what it's like to live without order or purpose. Ben thinks that his current life is a mess, but there's hope. It doesn't have to be like this.

A: Why did you show him that he was a horse?

M: There's no particular reason. Ben loves horses. I wanted to show him what it's like to be a horse.

A: Then you showed him that he was a black slave his entire life. Why?

M: Sometimes, Ben thinks he's inferior in relation to other people, and that he serves them in some capacity. Unlike the black slave that he was, he should know he has choices now. He doesn't have to be in that mentality and can choose whatever he wants. He can be what he wants, the one who is served *and* the one who serves.

A: In what context does he feel that he serves others?

M: He does things to make others pleased with him, love him and approve of him... as if what others think is more important than what he thinks.

A: Is that why he feels like he serves others?

M: Yes. Then he chose to be black. I wanted to show him that even now, if he feels that way, it is a choice. He doesn't have to feel that way.

A: When he was black, they were freed, but not much changed. Is there anything he should understand that's relevant to his life?

M: Real change must come from within. He must change whatever is seared into his brain. A change in feeling or in consciousness has to occur and not just in what he does or says. He has to change everything inside, literally. He simply has to understand that he's not less important than others in the world. Everyone has rights, like everybody else.

A: Why is it hard for him to understand that?

M: Somehow he is convinced that he's not good enough, and that others are better.

A: How can he change that?

M: He has to trust himself more. He has to say to himself all the time that he's not inferior to others.

A: *Next, you showed him that he was white with black slaves. Why?*

M: To let him know that these are two sides of the same coin. If he's the one being served, then he's the one that's considered the best. If he's the king of the world, it doesn't benefit him really. He doesn't gain anything and has no satisfaction. He must do things for himself in any case. He thinks that if people think he's very good, he'll feel good. Actually, it's not true. He has to feel good from within, and his worth cannot come at the expense of others or be relative to others. It must be absolute. He cannot feel good because others feel bad, and he cannot feel worthy because others feel inferior.

A: *So what would make him feel good?*

M: Trusting in himself, loving himself and not requiring approval or love from others.

A: *Not even love from others?*

M: Not even love from others. He must be his own master.

A: *So a person can feel good if he loves himself even if no one else loves him?*

M: Yes. He can love and rely on himself.

A: *Ben has a question: why does his heart still beat fast before events even though he knows nothing bad will happen?*

M: Ben is not connected to himself. His heart beats fast because of the residue of survival instincts. When humans experience danger, they either prepare for battle or run away. Their blood flows faster when trying to make decisions and respond quickly. That's how Ben's body reacts even though he knows there is no real danger. Because he's not connected to his body, it reacts independently. Ben has awareness and thoughts, but his body is not attuned to them. It's more like a reflex. He has no control. Control requires work and he doesn't do the work.

A: *What should Ben do?*

M: He should be aware of the situation when it happens and somehow calm himself. He needs to find ways to calm himself, and then his anxiety will gradually decrease and eventually stop. He should close his eyes and convince himself that everything is okay. This will calm him.

A: Ben has another question: why do people get offended?

M: Most people don't love themselves, so they need love from outside. It's their way to get attention, compassion and love. It's just an excuse. Instead of asking for love, they demand love. They try to take love by force from whoever offended them.

A: So a person who loves himself never gets offended?

M: It depends on how much he loves himself. No one loves himself completely.

A: Does it mean that the more a person loves himself the less he gets offended?

M: Yes, but he has to really love himself. It can't be a selfish, egocentric love. He must simply trust himself and love himself.

COMMENTARY

In this session Ben experienced both sides of a charged situation: he was a slave and then a slave owner. These are two sides of the same coin. In either case there is no growth or satisfaction in life. There is a mutual dependency that prevents real autonomy or self-sufficiency. A person has to take care of himself and not live his life as a servant to others or expect others to serve him.

Social status does not mean anything and the way one is perceived by others is not important. A person has to feel good from within, and self-worth cannot come at the expense of others or be relative to others. It must be absolute.

MESSAGES

1. Real change must come from within.
2. Everyone has the same rights to well-being and autonomy.
3. Self-worth cannot be relative to others; it must be absolute.

STUDY QUESTIONS

1. Do you depend on approval from others to feel good about yourself?

2. Can you identify a connection between getting offended and the need for love from others?

AFFIRMATIONS

1. I treat everyone with respect and compassion because I know that everyone is equally worthy.
2. I am worthy.

SESSION TEN

Projecting Pictures and Characters

DURING Ben's stay in the U.S., we had many discussions about the meaning of life and the sessions. He said he still wasn't sure that past lives were real, or that he wasn't making up the information in the sessions. I then suggested that he try to make up such stories in his normal state of awareness, without hypnosis. He tried for a while but came up with nothing.

Ben: I see a figure, a translucent blue figure. It's floating and projecting pictures. It's using a hand to continually project pictures in the air. I see images of people and places. All the time... figures going by quickly: *Tuk, tuk, tuk, tuk...* [making sounds]. I'm watching scenes from my lives; things and people I encountered.

Anat: What lives?

B: All my lives. I recognize some from Earth...

A: And from other places?

B: I recognize other places as well. There's a picture every second. *Tuk, tuk, tuk...* Figures. Maybe one of them is me?

A: Try to connect with the translucent figure. Ask about what you're seeing and the meaning behind it.

B: There's no talk between us.

A: No communication?

B: There is some knowledge, understanding... It's showing me my characters. It's all the people I interacted with. All this is to show me that there's nothing to fear.

A: Why is there nothing to fear?

B: Because it's all just characters, like in a movie. It's all for interaction in order to test how I behave.

A: Why is there a need to test that?

B: Because I wanted to check it out. It seemed interesting to me. It was my choice.

A: *What happens next?*

B: I'm still projecting these pictures all the time.

A: *What does it feel like seeing these pictures?*

B: Reassuring because there's nothing to fear.

A: *Now ask to stop the pictures at a place that will be interesting for you to see.*

B: I stop at my father's image.

A: *Your father now?*

B: Yes.

A: *What do you see?*

B: I see a picture of him. It's like a portrait. It's not a video; it's just a still picture.

A: *How do you feel seeing it?*

B: There are many emotions: anger, pity, love, understanding...

A: *Keep watching the picture until it changes to something that is important to see, or until you understand something about it.*

B: It shows me when I was young, about ten or eleven years old. I see anger, a lot of anger and fear. I see his anger and my fear.

A: *Keep watching until you understand what it means, and why it's important for you to see it now.*

B: It's to show me how I dealt with anger.

A: *How did you deal with anger?*

B: With fear.

A: *Now after seeing how you dealt with anger, keep looking until you understand what you're supposed to learn from it, or how it's relevant now.*

B: I understand now that sometimes people have to be angry either because they're afraid, or because that's how they are built. It's not about me.

A: *So his anger was not related to you?*

B: Related and unrelated at the same time.

A: *What else?*

B: I see a picture of my mother.

A: *What do you see there?*

B: Same thing.

A: *Also anger?*

B: Yes.

A: *And what do you make of it?*

B: Same thing.

A: *Keep looking until you understand how it's relevant to your life now.*

B: It helps me understand that people are a bit like machines. It's very difficult for them to control their emotions. They're not aware of what motivates them. I want to be aware of what motivates me in order to gain control.

A: *Keep looking until you understand what will help you become more aware and have more control.*

B: Remember now. Be aware of the pictures all the time because then the truth is understood. Everyone is a character. They're live characters with feelings, but for me they're still characters. Characters who come to show me things, test me, help me test myself and see how I respond to them.

A: *So basically you wanted the interactions with these characters?*

B: Yes.

A: *If you remember that, will it help you?*

B: Yes. If I'm interacting with someone, I can imagine that his picture is passing through in the background, along with the other characters in life, and he's just one of them. Like in a movie.

A: *Are you still seeing the pictures changing?*

B: Yes, all the time.

A: *Keep looking until something happens or until it stops on another relevant picture.*

B: I see a picture with black inside, like a tunnel. I'm entering the tunnel in the picture. Everything is dark and scary. I'm moving slowly, trying to grope around with my hands. I'm becoming anxious. I no longer remember where I came from and can't go back. I'm moving, and I don't know if I'll get out of there alive. My hands are scraped by the walls. I keep moving forward because I have no choice. I know that nobody will find me if I stay in one place; I must progress. There's a little moisture on the walls. Finally, I see a light and advance toward it. I'm able to exit at the end. I feel great relief. I go back to my tent. I have this tent in the field, and I go to sleep.

A: *What happens next?*

B: The pictures continue. It feels like I'm becoming one with the pictures. I change all the time. It feels chaotic. They are changing very quickly. I *am* the pictures; I contain them. Something like that. I can't get out of the pictures.

A: *Are you trying?*

B: Yes.

A: *What happens when you try?*

B: Nothing. I just can't. I can't understand them. I want to go to the cloud.

A: *Can you see the blue figure who was showing you the pictures in the beginning?*

B: Yes.

A: *Signal to the figure that you want to stop the pictures.*

B: They stopped. I extend my hand to him, and we hold hands. It feels good. He takes me to the cloud.

A: *May I speak with Ben's Mediator?*

Mediator: Yes.

A: *Why did you show Ben the pictures with the characters?*

M: To demonstrate that his entire life is built out of characters and they are not there to hurt him.

A: *So even if it seems like they hurt him, he shouldn't get hurt?*

M: True. They are only there to test him, entertain him and challenge him.

A: *Ben likes challenges?*

M: Yes.

A: *Did he choose to be in all those "movies"?*

M: Yes.

A: *You showed Ben that he was in a tunnel. It was very dark, and he knew he had to find the way out by himself. Why did you show him that?*

M: So that he always knows that wherever he is, and as dark and hopeless as it seems, there's always a way out. He can always find himself.

A: *There's always light at the end of the tunnel?*

M: Yes. All he needs to do is grope in the dark a bit, and in the end he will find his way.

A: *Then, he felt himself becoming the pictures, and it was hard for him to stop them and get out. Why did you let him experience that?*

M: To show him that everything he experiences is his own creation.

A: *Does this mean that he himself creates the stories he experiences?*

M: Yes.

A: *How does that explain the rest of the people? Do they also create their own stories even though they interact with Ben?*

M: Yes.

A: *So we all write the stories together?*

M: We are like neurons in one brain, the brain of all that exists.

A: *Ben asks why he would rather do easy things, like watch TV, rather than use his brain more actively.*

M: Because he doesn't trust himself. He thinks if he finds interest in other things, he would have to try them. He is afraid of failure.

A: *What can you suggest in that context?*

M: To look at things like steps without a definite purpose, without commitment. If he wants to change things for himself, he will. If he doesn't, then he won't. But it should not prevent him from moving forward.

A: *Ben still doesn't know if all these things are real. He doesn't know if the incarnations and the spiritual side of what we do are real. He doesn't even know if there's something beyond the physical world. He thinks he has no way of knowing.*

M: There's an answer, but he needs to go much deeper to find it.

A: *Is there anything that prevents him from going deeper?*

M: I don't know if there's anything that really prevents him. He sees sparks every time. He sees flashes of truth every once in a while, but he can't identify them because they're only momentary flashes. Somehow, he has to reach them.

A: Can our sessions help?

M: Yes.

A: Ben knows that he cares too much about what other people think about him, but it's not clear to him how to change that. Can you suggest anything?

M: He should remember the pictures from this session and remember that the characters aren't as real as they seem. Then, what they think will seem to be of no importance either.

A: Is there a reason for showing him pictures of his parents?

M: A lot of Ben's fear is affected by the past, so I show him that there's nothing to fear. There's no reason to fear anger because every person in this world is occupied with his own affairs more than the affairs of others. There's no point in investing energy in the affairs of others if they're angry or disappointed in you. They're occupied with themselves, not with you.

A: Is it possible that Ben's fears somehow prevent him from knowing the truth?

M: No. I think not. The truth, the discovery of truth is like being in a tunnel. Just feel around, and at the end you will find your way.

A: What does it mean to feel around in that context?

M: Think about the truth more. Imagine the truth. Imagine the flashes at the end that become a clearer picture.

A: Why is it so hard for people to love themselves?

M: It's easier for people to be loved by others.

A: Do you mean that it's easier for them to look for love in other people?

M: Not to look for love, to want love. People inherently look outside, not inward. They interact with the outside world, not their inner world; so it's easier for them to want things from the outside. One of these things is love. They're not aware of investing in love from within.

A: What can help people change that?

M: They need to be reminded that they are more than their external senses. They have a body, a heart, their own brain and their own self that they should take care of. Look within and not without.

A: Are people sometimes afraid to look within?

M: It's not that they're afraid... Their natural inclination is to look... They have to make an effort. All their senses are external, and their eyes are constantly looking outward instead of inward. So, their mind is constantly occupied with the outside, and they forget their inner world.

A: So in order to make it easier for people to love themselves, they should remember to look inside?

M: They need to look inside and close their eyes a lot.

A: To block the outside world?

M: Yes.

A: Many people use the external world to avoid looking inside.

M: It's much easier. You can look within using your eyes only if they're closed. Even then it's not easy. It's much easier to look outside because that's what eyes are for.

A: So that means meditation and time spent with the self?

M: Yes.

COMMENTARY

This session presents the idea that we choose to experience the events and interactions in our lives in order to challenge ourselves. Thus there is nothing to fear. We are not meant to be hurt by the experiences, but to be challenged by them and learn from them.

MESSAGES

1. Characters in your life exist in order to challenge you, and they cannot actually hurt your essence.
2. When others harbor some sort of negativity about you, they're occupied with themselves, not you.
3. You are more than your external senses, and you can take care of yourself by looking within and not without.

STUDY QUESTIONS

1. When you are upset with someone else, can you identify your internal motivation?
2. What would help you interact more with your inner world and less with the external one?

AFFIRMATIONS

1. My eternal soul is greater than any perceived hurt in this life.
2. I remain calm and peaceful while interacting with others because I know that I create my own experience.

SESSION ELEVEN

Gorilla's Guilt

SINCE we began focusing on the information that came through our sessions, Ben started reading a couple of books about human behavior. He had some questions about the material he was reading. We talked about people's tendency to focus on the negative aspects of situations instead of the positive ones.

In this session we asked to see the past life that is the most influential on Ben's current stage of life.

Ben: There are trees all around. We're a band of gorillas and I'm the leader. We're like a family with a female and two children. I always watch out for them in order to keep them safe. That is my purpose.

Anat: What does the female do? What is her role?

B: She teaches our children how to find food. They find insects, plants, and fruits on trees.

A: Move forward in time to a significant event in that life.

B: There are some people in the forest. I signal to everyone to get close to me. I climb a tree, look around and see hunters coming. Africans. I yell to warn everyone, but I'm too late. The hunters have already shot my family dead. They drag them away in chains. I try to approach without being seen. I know there's nothing I can do, and I feel awful. They're dead because I couldn't protect them. I didn't do my job even though I watched all the time. I thought I was protecting them by watching and occasionally scaring away animals in the forest. At the moment of truth, it didn't work. I couldn't protect them. I sit and wait in the woods alone. The clan, the larger group of gorillas, rejects me. My family was killed, so I become an outcast.

They won't accept large males who can't protect their family. I have become a burden.

A: So what do you do?

B: I'm alone in the woods, and there is nothing to do. I'm deeply depressed. I do nothing. All I do is look for food. I eat and sit. That's how I spend the rest of my life.

A: Move forward in time to the last day of your life.

B: I'm shot with an arrow. It's very painful. I see a few hunters with blow darts above me, looking at me. They're speaking in a language I don't understand. Then everything goes dark. I'm probably dead.

A: After you leave your body, what do you think?

B: I feel sorry for myself, for the gorilla that I was, because I was alone at the end. I didn't protect my family, and they were killed. It wasn't my fault that I couldn't protect them. Now I can see that it wasn't my fault. As a gorilla, I didn't know that. I thought it was my fault.

A: What happens next?

B: I decide to be someone of that tribe in Africa. I'm a small African child, about four or five years old. I play with other children. We live in huts. We play soccer with a ball made of plants and leaves that we tied together. Besides playing, we don't have too much to do. We don't have much to eat. We live in the jungle, and it's difficult to hunt animals. My father is one of the hunters in the village.

A: What kind of animals do they hunt?

B: Everything.

A: How do you feel there as a kid?

B: I feel good. I play whenever I want. I don't need much food so I'm not hungry a lot.

A: Move forward in time until a significant event happens in that life.

B: I wake up in the morning, and I hear mom and dad arguing. Dad says that he heard you can hunt gorillas and get paid a lot of money for their organs, arms, hands and head. My mother doesn't want my dad to hunt gorillas because they are too similar to humans to kill them. They keep arguing. My father is trying to persuade her that it's worth our while because he's tired of going hunting and working hard all the time. He also likes gorillas and monkeys, but he feels he has no choice. He's tired of working very hard.

A: *What do you think about it?*

B: I don't want him to hunt gorillas. I like all apes. I don't care that he'll work hard.

A: *So what happens at the end?*

B: Eventually, he convinces her. He doesn't really convince her, but he's the one who decides, so she has no choice but to accept it.

A: *Then what happens?*

B: For a while now, I see that we have more food, and he hunts less. So I want to go with him to see how it's done.

A: *How old are you now?*

B: Seven or eight. He says it's too dangerous because gorillas are very aggressive and one has to get closer to them than to other animals. He wants to wait a year or two until I can go with him. So we wait two years before I go with him on a hunt. He and several other men go. I'm the only child there. We walk quietly in the direction where we think the gorillas are. Suddenly, one of the men signals to everyone that he sees a band of gorillas. My father signals to me not to move. Everyone tries to walk slower and more quietly. My dad signals to me to advance a bit behind him very carefully and quietly, until we are close enough to see a clearing between the trees where a few gorillas are sitting. The young ones are playing with each other. My father signals me to look at what he does. He has a long blow dart. He takes a long arrow, not an arrow of archery, but a much smaller and thinner one. He dips it in poison, puts it in the blow dart, puts the blow dart in his mouth, inhales and directs it toward one of the gorillas there. He blows out all the air at once. The dart flies into one of the gorillas. The gorilla sighs, not of pain, more like it falls asleep. It falls off its feet and lies down. All the other gorillas begin to run wild and scream. Then I see that they also get shot by the rest of the hunters who came with us. After a few seconds, all the gorillas are lying on the ground with darts in their chest. Some of them are still alive and breathing heavily. The hunters take big rocks and hit them hard on the chest. They don't hit them on the head because it would spoil the gorilla. They deliver a very big blow to the chest to make the gorilla stop breathing. When all of them are dead, the hunters tie their legs and hands and drag them back into the woods.

A: *How do you feel seeing all that?*

B: I feel terrible about it. I decide that I don't want to go with my dad to hunt gorillas anymore. I don't want to see gorillas being killed even if it means I have more to eat.

A: *What happens next?*

B: I forget about all this business in the coming years.

A: *So, you're not going to hunt gorillas anymore?*

B: No. After a few years, I try to convince my father to stop hunting gorillas, but he refuses. He says it's the best way to survive since the value of gorillas increased in recent years due to fewer gorillas. I cry and want him to stop, but he doesn't want to hear of it. A few more years pass. I have a wife but no children. I decide to fight for those gorillas. I join the police.

A: *Is it illegal to hunt gorillas?*

B: A law forbidding gorilla hunting passed a couple of years earlier, but people don't abide by the law. Our unit catches the poachers.

A: *What happens to the hunters when they're caught?*

B: They go to jail for ten days, but that doesn't deter them. They continue to hunt, and we try to catch them in the act. We carry out raids in the forest, find bands of gorillas and ambush the hunters. It usually works. They usually go to jail for ten days or get a fine, but that doesn't deter them.

A: *Does anything else happen?*

B: One day we try an ambush. We lie down next to a band of gorillas. One gorilla is suddenly shot in the chest. We usually catch the hunters before they hurt the gorillas, but this time we are too late. I run to the gorilla and then feel something in my chest. I look left and see the hunter who shot me. He seems very surprised because he probably didn't mean to shoot me. Because of all the trees, he couldn't see too well and thought I was a gorilla. I see my friends, the policemen, arresting all the hunters who are shocked by my sight. I can hardly breathe, so three people pick me up and carry me back to the village. Because the gorillas are usually up in the mountains, it's a long way down. In the village there are some old people who heal by using herbs. Fortunately, the wound isn't fatal, so they are able to heal me. I decide to continue with this work because I felt what a gorilla feels when it's hurt. It felt worse than I thought, and to die is even more horrible. So I continue with the ambushes to fight the poaching.

A: *Move forward in time to the last day of that life.*

B: There's a plague in the village, and I'm very sick. I simply die.

A: *After you die and leave this life, what thoughts do you have about it?*

B: I feel pretty happy with that life. I did something good.

A: *May I speak with Ben's Mediator?*

Mediator: Yes.

A: *Why did you choose to show him that he was a gorilla?*

M: Because Ben is sometimes afraid to take responsibility, so I showed him a life where you can be responsible for others and for yourself. Even if something bad happens and it seems like you made a mistake and everything is your fault, it is not necessarily so. Sometimes there are things that are not under your control, and you do your best. That is good enough. The main thing is to do your best, no matter what the consequences are later.

A: *We asked to see the life that is the most influential on this stage of his current life. How is that life affecting him now?*

M: Because he was responsible for his family, and he saw them killed, it causes him to avoid responsibility. He's afraid that something bad will happen and that he's not good enough to be the one taking responsibility. We had to show him what happens afterward, to show him that objectively, it's not his fault. Because he watched over them so well, they were able to live until he could no longer protect them. The circumstances were stronger than him.

A: Is this the reason Ben doesn't have children now? He doesn't want to be responsible?

M: That too.

A: In what other ways does he avoid responsibility?

M: He prefers someone else to take responsibility even for the things he does. For example, at work, if he does something, he'd rather have someone else take responsibility.

A: So it's time to change that?

M: Yes, he should trust himself more. He should realize that it's enough to do his best. That's all. There's no need for more. The results don't matter.

A: Why did you show him the time he decided to be an African fighting against gorilla hunting?

M: When he was a gorilla, he wanted to know what happened on the other side, since he saw it as evil. We showed him that within the mantle of evil, there could also be good. Not everyone is bad even when it seems that way. When he makes generalizations, he should know that there are always exceptions.

A: So in that life, he was the exception because he was an African against hunting?

M: Yes.

A: Ben often has an experience and then decides he wants to know what it would be like on the other side, like when he was a king and then a thief. He was black and then white. Is it common for souls to experience both sides of a situation?

M: Yes, it is. It always happens. Experiencing one side opens many questions about the other side. To answer them, it's necessary to experience the other side.

A: Ben said that when he has to go abroad on a business trip, he has no desire to go; but if the trip is canceled, he's disappointed. We tried to understand why this happens.

M: When they first tell him to go, he thinks about all the negative moments that can happen on that trip. He looks at the trip in a negative way. Then, he starts to look at the positive things about the trip, like not having to go to work. It's a kind of freedom in some cases. So when they tell him he's not going, he feels like they're taking away his freedom and the positive moments.

A: In that context, it seems like we have a tendency to see the negative side of things rather than the positive one. Is this true?

M: Yes, it is. People focus on the negative because it gives them an excuse to look for energy from other people. They are constantly searching to fill holes in themselves because of their lack of self-love. They're looking for someone else to love them.

A: So the reason people see the negative in things is that they want an excuse to take energy from others?

M: Something like that.

A: Will people who work on themselves and love themselves be less inclined to see the negative things and see the positive ones more?

M: Yes. They don't need negative things as an excuse to get love. For those who love themselves, the holes fill by themselves.

A: So the solution is, again, self love?

M: It's a solution.

A: To have that, one should look inward, meditate, and all those things we talked about?

M: Yes.

A: Will it help to practice focusing on positive things rather than negative ones?

M: It can help for a limited time, but eventually you have to love yourself.

A: Recently, Ben read books suggesting that every decision is made in the subconscious before the person is consciously aware of it. Does that mean that there's no free will?

M: No, it doesn't. Because the amount of information that one receives is very large, the subconscious just gives a recommendation. It doesn't decide. The role of free will is to decide whether to accept the recommendation or not. Most people accept it without a second thought. People who want to be more aware of the matter can think back on the recommendation and decide whether or not to accept it. That's free will.

A: So in this sense, the subconscious is like a computer that calculates and then gives the result; and free will allows us to accept it or think about it again?

M: Yes. Most people don't have enough strength or energy to think about the recommendation, so they accept it.

A: According to the books Ben read, it seems like it's very easy to manipulate people. Why is that?

M: It goes back to the fact that people don't love themselves. If people don't love themselves, they look for energy from others. Then others can do whatever they want in exchange for that energy. People who don't love themselves are much more open to manipulation. A person who loves himself will know what's best for him a lot better than those who don't love themselves. The manipulations won't work as well.

A: Will it help the sessions if Ben intends to connect better, or believes that it's possible to connect?

M: Yes. When one believes, it is easier to connect.

A: Ben still has difficulty believing that, despite all the sessions we had. Why is that?

M: It seems to him that he can make things up anyway, so even if it's not true, the world can act as if it's true.

A: Do you have anything to say about that?

M: Believe it's true and then see what happens.

A: You'll see it when you believe it?

M: Yes.

A: When you answered the questions, you spoke in plural. You said: "We showed Ben" or "we wanted Ben". But I asked to speak with the Mediator. Is it significant that you said "we"?

M: It's the same thing.

A: So who did you mean by "we"?

M: We, as Mediators, who are everywhere. I can be seen as many.

A: So it's like you're separate, but essentially it's the same one?

M: It's like a brain with many modules.

A: Is it like the idea that people are not really separate, that we are all One?

M: Yes.

A: Before I bring Ben back, is there anything you'd like to say to him?

M: Be happier.

A: Can he choose to be happier?

M: Yes.

COMMENTARY

In this session Ben again experienced two sides of a situation. First, he was a gorilla and suffered the loss of his family. He blamed himself for their death because he was responsible for them. That experience is still affecting his current life, so he tends to avoid responsibility.

Then he had a life as an African man in a village where they hunted gorillas. He chose to be the exception and fight against poaching.

MESSAGES

1. Doing your best is what matters, not the results.
2. Within the mantle of evil, there could also be good.
3. There are always exceptions to generalizations.

STUDY QUESTIONS

1. If you knew you were likely to experience both sides of a situation, how might that affect your perception or behavior?
2. Do you sometimes choose to be miserable in order to get attention from others?

AFFIRMATIONS

1. Because I do everything to the best of my ability, I feel alive and happy.
2. I love myself; therefore I see the best in everything and everyone.

SESSION TWELVE

Merging Clouds

Ben was having trouble implementing suggestions from the Mediator and still felt troubled and unhappy. Despite repeated suggestions, he wasn't meditating at all.

In this session I directed him to experience an existence not on Earth.

Ben: I see before me all kinds of clouds in different colors: pink, blue, yellow, all colors. They are in front of me and on the sides. I don't see anything else besides clouds. I am also a cloud, a pink one.

Anat: What does it feel like to be a cloud?

B: I don't feel. There's only a desire to merge with other clouds.

A: What are you doing?

B: I'm moving forward. I'm approaching another cloud and trying to merge with it. It's not working.

A: What color is the other cloud?

B: Purple. We are permeating each other, but we still look like two different colors. We are not successful.

A: Is there any communication between you?

B: No. This is the communication, the merging.

A: How do you feel when you're unable to merge? Do you feel anything?

B: No. No. It just doesn't work and that's it.

A: What do you do next?

B: I separate; exit. We both get out of each other and then continue looking for other clouds to merge with. I keep moving, and then I find a cloud. We're not exactly clouds. We're like sprays. After spraying the air, there's a cloud of molecules that remain. We're like that but denser. Everyone has a different color. I find another cloud. It's yellow. I'm going into it, and we're trying to merge. It's not working. We each go on our separate ways. I keep searching and encounter a pink cloud.

A: *Same color as you?*

B: Yes. We're entering each other's domain, but again it's not working. It seems as if it is successful, but it's not. No, we don't succeed, so we separate. I continue again. I don't feel discouraged; I know that in the end I will find a cloud to merge with. I'm not worried. I keep moving. There's another cloud next to me. Blue, I think, light blue. We enter each other's domain and we're able to merge. We create a vortex or a type of vortex. We become a new color, purple, a shade of purple. Suddenly, I begin to feel things. All kinds of emotions: fear, hope, desire. As if I was born again. I now have a strong desire to merge again as well as fear that I won't be able to merge. All that I'm interested in is merging. I continue searching for more clouds to merge with.

Suddenly, I notice that there are clouds that seem to want to merge and others that do not. Actually, they want to, but they don't show it as much, as if they're afraid or unsure. I'm approaching those who want to merge. I encounter another cloud that seems to want to merge, and we have no problem. It's blue. We enter each other, manage to merge and become one. Again, there are emotions, but more powerful, of fear, a feeling of self, more self-awareness. Again, all I want is to merge. I notice that all those who look like they don't want to or want to, but are afraid, are those that have already merged to become like me. It seems that those who merged developed fear and emotions that interfere with merging. Gradually, there are more like that than there are ones that haven't merged yet and don't mind merging. They are the ones that everyone tries to merge with. Everybody tries to merge with them before they are all gone. So this process continues. I merge only with those who have never merged before. Each time, it gets a little scarier to merge, and there are more emotions that keep changing, between good and bad, suddenly good, then bad, then good, then bad, continually. Besides these clouds, I don't see anything. Everything is white, white background, all white. This seems to be some kind of a white plane. We're in the air. We are moving in an infinite white surface. Maybe it's a white planet, but there's nothing here other than white and colorful clouds.

A: What happens next, after you merge many times?

B: I can no longer find those that are easy to merge with. All of those have been merged. Then, we begin to try to merge with each other and it's not easy. We all examine each other. Should I, shouldn't I, what will I gain? Will I disappear or won't I? It's scary and not scary at the same time. In the end, no one is merging anymore because it's too scary. We constantly think about whether or not to merge. We don't know what to do. Everything is so scary, really scary.

A: Why?

B: We don't know what comes next. Perhaps our selves will be lost. Maybe we'll die in this process. How can it be that two who merge, end up as one, and both live? All these thoughts and emotions are constantly there. I don't know what to do. Basically we're just examining each other, like dogs sniffing each other and doing nothing. That's all we do.

A: Move forward in time until something else happens.

B: I decide that there's no choice, and I have to merge. I move towards other clouds and forcefully, I succeed. Despite all the fears, I force myself and notice that I'm still me, and that nothing has changed. Nothing has changed, but I'm less afraid to merge. I feel more centered and know more. I know that nothing bad will happen after I merge. I know the difference between right and wrong. I know how to discern when it will be all right and when it won't.

A: What happens next?

B: I keep merging. Every time I know more and have more confidence. I know what I'm doing is right, so I keep merging until there is no one left to merge with. I am the last one. What will I do now...?

A: So what will you do now?

B: I feel that I got everything I needed out of the experience. I already have endless confidence, so I decide to try to get back to the way it was because there's nothing left to do. I decide to die somehow and explode, to burst into pieces or fragments of clouds and return to the beginning. I do some sort of... not exactly meditation... Somehow I manage to calm my thoughts and relax, so I split. I split into millions of clouds.

A: What does it feel like?

B: It's kind of a relief. Now there's a goal, we have to merge.

A: What do you look like now? Are you one of those clouds, or everyone?

B: I'm probably one.

A: Then what happens? Does the entire process start again?

B: Yes.

A: Do you remember what happened?

B: I feel like I remember. I seem to know that it happened, but I don't feel it. I don't know if the rest of the clouds know it. Maybe the others know exactly like me because we all came out of one self?

A: Leave the clouds behind. Go to another time, another place.

B: I see green vegetation and trees. There are spiders.

A: What do you look like?

B: I don't know. I'm invisible.

A: What are the spiders doing?

B: Walking. They are round and have eight legs. They're stomping loudly on the ground.

A: How big are they?

B: About three to five feet. I see about three, four, five, six spiders... They are brown and yellow. For some reason they are stomping on the ground with their feet.

A: Where are you watching them from?

B: From above. I see that they're banging on the ground. Suddenly large worms emerge from the ground, and the spiders are eating them. I feel compassion for the worms. The spiders are only interested in eating them.

A: What happens next?

B: Nothing.

A: What are you doing? Just observing?

B: Yes.

A: Can you move around?

B: Yes, I'm hovering. I don't know what I am, but I'm hovering.

A: *Move forward in time until something happens.*

B: That's it. I'm leaving this place. I'm going to the cloud...

A: *May I speak with Ben's Mediator?*

Mediator: Yes.

A: *Why did you show Ben that he was a cloud?*

M: So that he won't think too much. He thinks that if he considers things in their entirety, he'll make the most correct decision. Usually when you think less and flow, the results are much better.

A: *How is that related to the clouds he saw?*

M: The clouds had a goal and had no problem achieving it because they knew they would succeed in the end. They were not afraid of failure. They knew that one just has to try and that's it. Everything works out. When they acquired knowledge and emotions, they held them back. Then, the same exact goal became complicated. Not because it really was complicated, but because they made it complicated.

A: *Did emotions and thoughts make it complicated?*

M: Yes, and fear.

A: *What caused that fear?*

M: Knowledge. Knowledge of what happens next.

A: *Is that also what Ben thinks about? Does he worry too much about the future?*

M: Yes.

A: *Is the solution to simply do and not think too much?*

M: That would be ideal, but people have to think. They have to know that thoughts have a certain place. It's okay to have them and to perceive them as something that exists, but not as motivation.

A: *Can you give an example of something that Ben thinks about too much instead of flowing with it?*

M: When he has to talk to new people, he thinks too much.

A: *After he merged many times, he had more confidence. What does that mean?*

M: There's a stage when there's no confidence. But if something is done enough times, the thoughts and feelings adjust in the end. If you have enough experience, conscious thoughts are simply in harmony with reality and there's confidence.

A: *At the end, he became one single cloud and decided to start all over again. What does that mean?*

M: There was no longer a challenge, so he wanted to start from scratch.

A: *Is there a need for a challenge in this life too?*

M: Yes.

A: *We asked to see life in a place other than Earth. This existence as a cloud, is it something he really experienced?*

M: Yes.

A: *It sounds like existences in various forms and situations are basically ways to learn how to be. Is that true?*

M: They are not ways to learn how to be. They're examples of how one *can* be. If one wants to be something, he or she can. It's a way to show him how to be what he wants to be.

A: *Why did you show him spiders eating worms?*

M: Ben just observed a planet and thought about whether or not to be there. He decided in the end not to because it seemed to him he didn't have much to learn from that experience. It didn't mean anything.

A: *So he saw different lives on various planets and could decide whether he wanted to be there or not?*

M: Yes.

A: *In the last session, you told Ben to be happier. We talked about it, but Ben doesn't know how. Can you help him with that?*

M: He should make an effort to focus on positive things. It's hard, but it will work.

A: *Why is that so hard?*

M: Returning to self-love...

A: *But is it possible?*

M: Yes. He needs discipline.

A: *I think that he finds it hard to be happy because he has no children. If he has children, will it help him be happy?*

M: It will help him at certain times to be happy.

A: But that does not mean he cannot be happy even now, regardless?

M: Right. He can be.

COMMENTARY

In this session, a different type of existence is described. Many clouds, each with an individual awareness, participated in a process of merging together to become a single being with a single consciousness. After the goal was accomplished, the entire process started again.

MESSAGES

1. Think less, flow more, and the results will be better.
2. With experience, thoughts adjust and there's more confidence.
3. To be happier, focus on the positive things in your life.

STUDY QUESTIONS

1. Do you tend to overthink things?
2. Do you take responsibility for your own happiness?

AFFIRMATIONS

1. I am confident in my ability to achieve my goals because I am learning to believe in myself.
2. I am looking forward to new challenges and the joy they bring into my life.

SESSION THIRTEEN

Killing Her Brain

Ben was still troubled by feelings of uncertainty about his girlfriend. He wasn't sure whether he wanted to take the next step with her or break up. He wasn't sure he loved her enough.

This session was conducted at night during a thunderstorm, which served as a fitting background. There are some elements of a horror story and graphic descriptions in this session. It could be read as a metaphor that teaches an important lesson.

Ben: I'm a man in the woods. There are many trees and a cabin. I don't know whether to go into the cabin. I know I should, but I'm afraid to enter because I'm afraid of what's inside.

Anat: Do you know what's inside?

B: Not exactly. I decide to go into the cabin. I open the door and step inside. I think it's my house. I'm looking around and there's a bed, a kitchen... Everything is made of wood. There's a small table lamp that's lit. There are cabinets and bottles of wine on the shelves. The cabin isn't that big and there's no one here. I sit on the bed.

A: How do you feel being there?

B: Safe. There is no one here. I recall that I had a wife. I have a feeling that she's with me, but she's not. I have a feeling that she's in the house, but she's not. There's a door in the floor to the cellar. I'm looking at the door, and I don't know whether or not to open it. I'm afraid to go down to the cellar because I know there are things there that will make me feel bad. I know I can't feel good about myself as long as I don't go down there, so I decide to go down anyway. I open the door and there's light. I go downstairs and see a body. I know it's my wife's body.

A: How do you feel seeing it?

B: It's very painful. Somehow I know it's my fault she's dead. Next to the body there's a jar. It's disgusting... Her brain is in the jar. The entire body is decomposing because it's been there for a long time, and I haven't been taking care of it. I've done nothing to preserve the body, but I did place the brain in chemicals. I know I have to bury them both.

A: *Your wife and her brain?*

B: Yes. I have to let them go, her...

A: *What do you do next?*

B: I decide to bury the body first. I wrap her in sheets and carry her up the stairs. She's not heavy because her body decayed and lost some weight. I take her to the forest. I dig a hole and bury the body inside. Then, I go home because the brain is there. Dealing with the brain is more difficult for me. The brain is my wife. Her body is just her body. The brain is her. I take the brain and look at it inside the jar. I try to talk to the brain.

A: *What are you saying?*

B: "I loved you... I didn't mean... I didn't mean for you to be in this situation. I didn't mean to kill you." I don't know if she can hear me. Maybe my voice is reaching the brain somehow, but she can't talk. She has no mouth and no head. I don't know what to do; maybe she's not dead. I convince myself that she's dead, and that the brain can't live without a body or electrical impulses or something to nourish it. I want to bury her, but I can't because if I'm wrong, I'll bury her alive. I decide to kill her again. But how do I kill her again? I can burn her, but it will hurt if she has awareness. What can I do? I can cut her with a knife, but that will also hurt. I don't know what to do... I don't know what to do... It has to be something quick and lethal. I decide to run over her. I have a truck. I put her on the road and decide to drive over her fast. I do it. Then I rinse her brain with water, spreading it with soil. This way I'm sure it's no longer alive. I feel a bit relieved because now I'm sure she is dead. I go back to the cabin; I take out a glass of wine and drink.

A: *What events led to the death of your wife?*

B: I remember the hand... knife in her chest.

A: *Do you mean that you had a knife in your hand, and you stabbed her in the chest?*

B: Yes. I thought she didn't love me anymore. She wasn't paying attention to me anymore. She no longer told me she loved me.

A: *Did you talk to her about it?*

B: No. It seemed natural that she didn't love me.

A: *Why did it seem natural?*

B: Not because it was my fault, but because of her behavior. She no longer cared about me.

A: *How did you feel about her?*

B: I loved her.

A: *What led to the decision to kill her?*

B: I saw no other choice. I wanted to punish her because she didn't love me anymore.

A: *How did you feel after she died?*

B: I felt that now I was loved even less. I wanted her to love me again, so I opened her head and took out her brain. I thought that's how I would have access to her love; I'd go straight to the source. Then, I began to realize that it didn't work that way, and she couldn't love me anymore. I didn't know if she was alive or not. I didn't feel that she loved me, and that her brain could love me. There was no response. I decided to keep her in the cellar so that no one would see, and somehow, she would still be with me. So I kept her. I kept the brain in a jar with chemicals. I knew what I was doing wasn't normal, but I couldn't act differently. Somehow, I got into my head that I had to have her stay with me, and that I must preserve her. On the other hand, it doesn't work like that, so I decided to bury her.

A: *Go back to the moments after you buried her, and you're drinking wine. How do you feel now?*

B: I feel guilty. Guilty that I did what I did and saw things the way I saw them. I don't understand how I could do such a thing, or how I could think that way.

A: *So it doesn't seem to make sense now?*

B: No, absolutely not.

A: *What do you decide to do next?*

B: I decide to commit suicide. I take a lot of sleeping pills because I can't stand myself.

A: *What are your last thoughts?*

B: That I'm bad.

A: *What happens after you take the sleeping pills?*

B: I fall asleep.

A: *Move forward in time until after you separate from your body. What are your thoughts?*

B: Guilt. Even when I'm out of my body I feel guilty.

A: *Do you decide anything about your next life?*

B: I decide to always see both sides, not just my side.

A: *May I speak with Ben's Mediator?*

Mediator: Yes.

A: *Why did you choose to show Ben this life today?*

M: Because Ben often thinks of himself and not others. He doesn't pay attention to others or their needs, so I showed him how it feels, and where it can lead.

A: *Are there certain situations when he doesn't think of others?*

M: His girlfriend. He doesn't show that he cares. He's too busy with his own issues. He needs to know that it's not how you're supposed to behave.

A: *What can he do differently?*

M: He should be more aware of his behavior and try to make an effort to change.

A: *Does he care?*

M: Yes.

A: *So why doesn't he show it?*

M: Because he's preoccupied with his lack of self-love.

A: *He said he's not sure whether he loves her or not. How is that related?*

M: He won't know if he loves her until he tries to love her, until he can show her that he loves her. He doesn't let himself show it because he's preoccupied with himself. He can show her that he loves her, and then he'll know.

A: Shouldn't he already know that he loves her in order to show her?

M: No. He should act like he loves her, and then he will know.

A: What else can help him be less preoccupied with his lack of self-love?

M: He should pay attention to others. Then he'll feel better about himself.

A: If he expresses love to others, like his girlfriend, will it help him love himself more?

M: Yes.

COMMENTARY

This session depicts a disturbing story of murder from the perpetrator's point of view. The lesson of the story might seem anticlimactic. A horrible act was committed and the lesson is: don't think of yourself only; think of others too. Why such a disturbing story to convey such a simple message? Or is this lesson more significant than it seems at first? It is a story about the consequences of not having empathy. The perception that others exist in order to fulfill one's own needs is dangerous. In this story it led to murder. Perhaps metaphorically it shows how important empathy is. Lack of it might not lead to murder in most cases, but it robs the other person of the right to exist as a separate human being with feelings and needs.

MESSAGES

1. It is not possible to change another person's feelings by force.
2. Paying attention to others and being considerate will make you feel good about yourself.

STUDY QUESTIONS

1. Do you show enough love and appreciation to the people close to you?
2. Are you aware of other people's needs in addition to your own?

AFFIRMATIONS

1. The more love I express toward others, the more loved I feel.
2. I am considerate of other people's feelings and needs, therefore I experience harmony in my life.

SESSION FOURTEEN

Bubbles in a Wall

BEN and I were having discussions about messages from the sessions. He was finding it difficult to apply them to his everyday life.

Ben: I see a gray wall, an endless wall. I don't know what it's made of, but there are bubbles of glass in it. There's something in each bubble, some kind of lightning bolt. They're on and changing all the time.

Anat: What do you look like?

B: I have no body.

A: What does it feel like looking at the lightning bolts inside the bubbles?

B: Like obstacles. Those lights are my thoughts. I try to touch them.

A: What happens when you touch them?

B: I get an electric shock every time. I try to pass through the bubbles in order to advance, but I can't.

A: Do you know what's behind the wall?

B: No.

A: Do you see the edges of the wall?

B: No. I just see a wall full of bubbles with lights. These are my thoughts. I'm trying to pass through, and I can't because I'm thinking thoughts that stop me. It's as if I'm driving the wall.

A: Do your thoughts drive the wall? Do they provide energy to the wall?

B: Not exactly energy... The wall doesn't need energy. Simply put, the energy is in the glass bubbles, and when they're on, I can't go through.

A: Focus for a moment and see if you can turn them off or weaken them.

B: I'm trying to look for a bubble to focus on. Everything's a mess. I keep thinking and can't focus on the bubble.

A: Concentrate on one bubble and tell me what happens.

B: I approach a bubble and try to figure out which thought keeps it running. It's the thought that I'm not smart enough.

A: What can you do to change that bubble?

B: I'm trying to think that I'm smart enough, but I can't. I can't think that. I keep thinking that there are others smarter than me, so that belief won't let me think that I'm smart enough. I can't think of myself without comparing.

A: Look for another bubble and find out what it says.

B: I approach a bubble. That bubble is the thought that I'm not making progress in life.

A: What do you want to do with it?

B: I try to think that I'm making progress, but I'm not able to think that. I think about other people. It seems to me that they're making progress and I'm not. So I'm trying to find another bubble. There are so many bubbles. I approach another bubble. What's this bubble? This bubble is the thought that all is physical and finite. This is a bubble that I manage to weaken. The light weakens, so I can turn it off.

A: Look behind the bubble and see what's behind the wall.

B: I see black behind the bubble.

A: Can you pass through this hole in the wall?

B: No, it's too small.

A: How can you enlarge it?

B: I have to look for other bubbles. I look around, but there are so many bubbles that I don't know where to go.

A: Is there anything that's close to the last bubble, so you can enlarge the hole? Maybe you can choose a bubble that's close, to be able to widen the opening.

B: Okay. I'm looking at a bubble next to it. This is the bubble of my thoughts when I talk and sing to myself sometimes.

A: How can you weaken the lightning in that bubble?

B: I have to stop thinking.

A: *Stop thinking for a moment and see what happens. Clear your mind and look at the wall.*

B: The light stops and starts every time. On and off, like a broken fluorescent bulb. I'm not entirely successful.

A: *Maybe you should look for another bubble? What is the next bubble?*

B: This is a bubble of the past.

A: *What should be done to turn it off?*

B: Stop thinking about the past. I'm trying to stop thinking about the past... It turns off and the lightning stops.

A: *Is the hole bigger now?*

B: No, the bubbles are not touching each other. It's like a lattice.

A: *What do you see behind that bubble?*

B: Black. I'm trying to insert my arm through the bubble, but only my hand goes through.

A: *Do you feel anything behind?*

B: I don't feel my hand when it's behind the wall.

A: *Do you feel it when it's in front of the wall?*

B: Yes.

A: *So now you have a body?*

B: I feel I have a body, but I can't see it.

A: *What do you want to do now?*

B: I want to get through to the other side.

A: *What do you need to do in order to get to the other side?*

B: Continue to look for large bubbles.

A: *Look and find the bubble that seems the largest.*

B: I see a large bubble. What thought is this bubble? It's the thought of the self as singular, as something separate from the universe.

A: *What do you need to do in order to turn off that bubble?*

B: I need to remember. I have to remember that I'm part of the universe, part of everything. I remember that I'm part of everything. The bubble disappears. I'm being sucked into the bubble, into the wall. I'm becoming that wall. I can control all the bubbles and turn on and off any bubble I want. I can think what I want. I have complete control over my thoughts, and it feels great.

A: *Are you choosing new thoughts?*

B: Yes, I'm turning them on and off. One moment I choose to think I'm smart, and the next I stop that thought. Another time I choose to think I'm stupid, and then stop that thought too. I choose to know everything... I choose to know nothing... Whatever I choose, I believe it and know it because I see that everything is actually thought. All of it is interpretation. I have endless bubbles... I have endless bubbles...

A: *What's happening now?*

B: I keep turning thoughts on and off. I'm trying to turn emotions on and off, but I can't. I can control only thoughts.

A: *What controls emotions?*

B: I don't know.

A: *Are emotions also bubbles?*

B: No. There are no emotions. I'm looking for emotions...

A: *Can you find them?*

B: No. I'm trying to continue with the bubbles, to see if they cause emotions. I find that there are feelings of fear when certain bubbles are turned on and off.

A: *What bubbles, for example?*

B: When I turn on the bubbles that make me think I know everything, I think I know everything, but I don't. There's a feeling of anxiety because there's a thought that I know everything, but I don't really. On the one hand, I know that I know everything. On the other hand, I don't know what the bubbles of fear are. This contradiction makes me anxious. I'm beginning to understand that when there is a contradiction, there is emotion. I think something, I understand it's not true, but I still think it. It makes me anxious. Maybe this is the way I'll find out what causes fear. Yes, it makes me afraid and stressed. I know something and I don't understand it. It causes fear. I'm less scared now because I realized this.

A: *What happens next?*

B: I decide to leave the wall.

A: *To go where?*

B: There is only one way, where I came from. There's nothing behind the wall. I go back to the cloud...

A: *May I speak with Ben's Mediator?*
Mediator: Yes.
A: *Why did you show him the wall?*
M: I wanted him to know that everything is thought. All perceived limitations are only thoughts. There's nothing else besides thoughts.
A: *Is the physical world also made of thoughts?*
M: The physical world is energy. Thoughts are the interpretation of that energy.
A: *How can he control his thoughts in order to live better?*
M: He needs to understand that everything is thought. Once he really understands and knows it, everything will be very easy. He needs to always keep in mind that everything is thought.
A: *So what are emotions?*
M: Emotions are discrepancies between thoughts and truth. If he sees something that doesn't fit his beliefs, it causes some type of emotion, perhaps fear. If he knows something, and he believes in something else, two parts of him know different things, and it causes some negative emotion.
A: *How can it be resolved so that the negative emotions are overcome?*
M: Face the fact that everything exists and everything happens. Even if there are two things that apparently contradict each other, they don't really. They're different sides of the same coin, actually. He should understand that everything is true, one Truth, even if it doesn't seem that way. Everything happens and everything makes sense.
A: *What causes positive emotions?*
M: The process of understanding that everything exists.
A: *Are you saying that thoughts cause emotions?*
M: Yes, but thoughts in plural, not a single thought. A negative emotion can only be caused by a few thoughts together at the same time.

A: Can a single thought cause a positive emotion?

M: It's not exactly a thought. It's an understanding; true understanding.

A: Of the truth?

M: Yes.

A: Why is it so difficult for us to accept the truth?

M: Because there are many thoughts, and it's difficult to think one true thought. There are so many thoughts in parallel that it's hard to silence them and reach an understanding.

A: In order to reach an understanding, do thoughts have to be silenced?

M: Yes. One needs to focus on the basic understanding that everything happens and all is Truth.

A: Why does that understanding help us to feel good?

M: Because there's no reason to feel bad. One feels either good or bad. Once you understand that everything is true, there's no contradiction between thoughts because everything is fine and is supposed to happen.

A: Then even things that we consider bad are supposed to happen and that's okay?

M: Yes.

A: So when that is understood we feel good?

M: Yes.

A: Ben and I had a conversation yesterday about how hard it is to adhere to these understandings. Ben said that he has to focus and repeat the ideas to himself constantly. It's a very difficult and long process.

M: He's right. It takes a lot of work.

A: But it's possible?

M: Yes.

A: Can Ben do it?

M: If he makes the effort...

A: Does he have to make an effort to do it?

M: Everyone has to.

A: Is there a way to shorten that process?

M: No. Everything depends on the right amount of concentration.

A: So, the more one focuses on it the faster it happens?

M: Yes, self-discipline.

A: Is it possible to reach that understanding fully as human beings?

M: It can be reached, but it will be forgotten. We constantly have to be reminded of it.

A: Why is that? Why are we built like that?

M: It's just the way it is...

A: While Ben, or his being, is on the colorful planet, is it easier than this?

M: The colorful planet is... That is it. The beings there don't have to be reminded; the memory is always there.

A: So on the colorful planet it's not an issue that there is one Truth?

M: Right.

A: So do you mean that when we're born on other planets, it's difficult because we don't remember?

M: Yes.

A: Do we remember more after we die, and we're no longer connected to a body?

M: After you die, you know everything. If you go to the colorful planet, you'll know.

A: Do we always go to the colorful planet after death, or do we sometimes remain on Earth to live another life?

M: You always return to the colorful planet. You might go back to Earth, but everything goes through the colorful planet.

A: When we die, do we automatically return to the colorful planet every time?

M: Yes.

COMMENTARY

This session demonstrates the idea that all is thought. By controlling our thoughts better, we can have more control over our lives and the way we feel. Our thoughts and beliefs dictate our feelings, all of which can be changed.

MESSAGES

1. All is thought.
2. Everything exists and everything happens.
3. Contradictions between beliefs and truth cause negative emotions.

STUDY QUESTIONS

1. What self-limiting beliefs do you have that you would benefit from changing?
2. What thoughts might be in your way to true understanding?

AFFIRMATIONS

1. I choose to free my mind from limitations and difficulties and embrace infinite possibilities.
2. I am part of the universe, part of everything; therefore all is well in my life.

SESSION FIFTEEN

Trapped on a Spaceship

D URING Ben's stay in the U.S., he wasn't always in the mood for a
session, but sometimes we conducted one anyway. Likewise,
the following session took some effort on his part.

Ben: I'm in a spaceship. I see yellow-gray corridors.
Anat: What do you look like?
B: I'm wearing a blue overall. I think I'm a man.
A: Is there an insignia on your overall?
B: There's a patch in the shape of a star, in white.
A: Are there any other people?
B: At the moment I'm alone, but there are other people on board.
A: What are you doing?
B: I walk into a room. I see a chair and electrodes. I have to sit
there and plug into the chair. I sit down in the chair, put a helmet
over my head and press a button. I hear buzzing. Suddenly I can't
think of anything. It feels like this machine is draining all the energy
from me, sucking my brain. I think it's energy for the spacecraft.
After half an hour I stop it, or it stops by itself.
A: How do you feel when it stops?
B: Relieved.
A: Is there any change in the spaceship?
B: No.
A: Can you see outside from this room?
B: No. It's a small room, maybe a little bigger than an airplane
lavatory.
A: What do you do next?
B: I go outside, walk down the hall and see people in other rooms.
I also see people walking, but they're not talking.

A: Can you see outside the spaceship?

B: No. I don't know why I think it is a spaceship. I know it's a spaceship, but there are no identifying characteristics. There are only corridors and people in small rooms. There are some people who are not plugged in.

A: Where do you see people who are not plugged in?

B: In the corridors. There are rooms without chairs, and people are standing there.

A: What are they doing?

B: Nothing, just standing. I feel no need to talk to them.

A: What do you want to do now?

B: I want to escape. I feel like a slave.

A: Is there a way for you to escape?

B: I don't know of one, but I must find a way.

A: Move forward in time to a significant event in that life.

B: I'm in some type of a control room. I don't know how I got here. The entire room is full of displays. On the displays, there are various colored circles. They can be touched and moved. There are lines between the circles.

A: What happens when you touch and move them?

B: I can connect the circles with the lines.

A: What happens when you do that?

B: I don't know.

A: Is there anyone else in the room?

B: No.

A: How do you feel being there?

B: No feeling. I'm trying to figure out what to do, how to use the circles to escape. Maybe if I connect the circles, I can escape. I'm trying to understand these circles. There are circles that have purple lines coming out of them, going to the rest of the circles. I think these circles represent the small rooms. I delete the lines between them. Nothing happens. I'm trying to figure out what to do. I don't know...

A: What can you do?

B: Somehow, I think I need to reverse the direction of the energy. Instead of having the energy drained out of us into the spaceship, it can give the energy back. I start to reverse the lines, but it doesn't work. I can't get the energy back. I'm still imprisoned. I don't succeed.

A: *Move forward in time until you succeed, give up, or something happens.*

B: I decide to go back to the little room. I go back, plug into the chair, press the button, and I don't get out until I die. All the energy is drained.

A: *Now that you ended your life, you realize what that life was about... When it becomes clear, tell me.*

B: I was a man who couldn't control his own thoughts. He was controlled by something else. He was controlled by his brain.

A: *A man who was controlled by thoughts of his own brain?*

B: Yes. It killed him.

A: *What was the spaceship?*

B: It was actually also a man in the universe, a type of spacecraft that did not move anywhere really. It drew the strength from the man and moved without control or purpose.

A: *What were the other people in the spaceship?*

B: They were desires that were also sucked into the thoughts, or the brain. They had no more energy because the thoughts were in control.

A: *What was the purpose of that life? Why did you have to experience it?*

B: He who is controlled by his brain dies eventually.

A: *One that is not controlled by his brain does not die?*

B: He dies, but later, later.

A: *Do you know how you got to that spacecraft?*

B: No. I don't remember how I got there.

A: *Now that you left your body, you can remember anything you want. Connect to how you got there, the beginning of that experience. When you know how you got there, tell me.*

B: I had to get there.

A: *What do you mean? Why did you have to?*

B: I felt like I had to give my energy away even though I didn't have much.

A: *Why did that feeling make you get there?*

B: Because it's easy, getting there, giving energy to the brain.

A: *Why is it easy?*

B: Because there is no need to do anything.

A: *Why did you want to escape from there?*

B: Because that process of transferring energy is painful, and it leaves you with nothing, so there's a desire to restore that energy.

A: *To get it back?*

B: Yes. It becomes a conflict.

A: *What was the significance of the control room with the purple circles and lines?*

B: There's always a way to turn it around.

A: *What do you mean turn it around?*

B: To stop the process of transferring energy, to get it back.

A: *So there's always a way?*

B: Yes.

A: *But you couldn't find the way?*

B: No.

A: *May I speak with Ben's Mediator?*

Mediator: Yes.

A: *Can you summarize the meaning of the experience you showed Ben?*

M: Ben had difficulties getting into the experience, so he created an experience that represented the process, where he tried and failed.

A: *Do you mean that he was unable to connect to something real that happened, so he created something that symbolized his difficulty; what he was trying to connect to?*

M: It's not that he was unable to connect to something real. He felt that his brain was in control, and he couldn't do anything.

A: *Do you mean during the session or in general?*

M: During the session.

A: *What is the meaning of that experience in that context?*

M: Most of the time, awareness is made of thoughts, and they need to be cleared from one's mind in order to get to the Truth.

A: *Is it difficult for Ben to do that?*

M: Yes.

A: *Can you explain why Ben said that anyone who thinks dies eventually?*

M: Anyone who thinks without control dies eventually.

A: *Do thoughts drain energy from a person? Do they cause him to lose energy?*

M: Not exactly lose energy, but the universe decides that he is no good; he's not needed. If he is an automaton, the universe doesn't need him. He serves no purpose.

A: *What purpose does a non-automatic person who controls his own thoughts serve?*

M: The purpose of an experience. A person who thinks automatically doesn't experience anything.

A: *But even a person who thinks automatically has feelings.*

M: Yes, but if the feelings are negative, in a sense, and they're always the same, then there's no need for that experience.

A: *Does that mean that people who live automatically, like robots, live less time than people who are more creative?*

M: They live less time in relation to themselves. If they weren't robots, they would have longer lives, relative to themselves.

A: *So it's like the universe is looking for new experiences all the time, and if they're always stuck in one experience, there's no point in continuing. Something like that?*

M: Something like that.

A: *Does that mean that people have to be creative and not automatons in order to serve a purpose?*

M: Not exactly creative. They need to control their thoughts better. They don't need to create all the time. They shouldn't let their brain control them.

A: *Is one's brain separate from one's awareness?*

M: No, the brain is part of awareness, but it can take over.

A: *So awareness has to control the brain and not vice versa?*

M: Yes.

A: *How can it be done?*

M: By observing thoughts from the outside. It takes self-discipline and practice.

A: Does it mean that a person who is aware of his thoughts, observes them from the outside and has more self-awareness, leads a more rewarding or valuable existence?

M: Yes.

A: Do we sometimes choose existences in which we have no control over our thoughts?

M: Yes.

A: Why do we choose them?

M: To make life more interesting, to overcome something.

A: So it's a challenge?

M: Yes.

COMMENTARY

In this session there is another discussion about the importance of controlling thoughts. It is easy to spend energy on thoughts that drain energy and are not productive. People should not let their brain control them or their experience.

MESSAGES

1. Thoughts need to be cleared from the mind in order to get to the Truth.
2. Awareness has to be in control, not the brain. Observe thoughts from the outside.
3. It takes self-discipline and practice to be able to observe thoughts from the outside.

STUDY QUESTIONS

1. Do you have repetitive thoughts that don't serve a purpose?
2. Are you able to observe your thoughts from the outside and not be controlled by them?

Affirmations

1. I feel calm and detached as I observe my thoughts.
2. I am the master of my own mind and consciously decide what to focus on.

SESSION SIXTEEN

The Power of Thoughts

B EN didn't have specific questions for this session, so we decided to just see what happened.

Ben: I'm a man wearing leather clothes. I'm walking in the woods. Ahead of me and behind me there are other people walking. We're carrying backpacks and walking with a purpose; I don't know where we're going yet.

Anat: Are you talking?

B: No.

A: Keep walking until something happens, or until you arrive.

B: We arrive at a construction site. There are more people there. There's a hole in the ground with a ladder in it. Someone meets us and says: "You're finally here." We nod our heads. Then, he points to the hole with his finger and tells us to go in. We climb down the ladder. The walls are damp. We continue down to the bottom. It's dark, but we have flashlights. We go inside a cave. There's an underground path we walk on. Sometimes it's a path, and sometimes we have to climb over rocks. We keep going down, and it feels like we've been walking for hours.

A: Do you talk among yourselves?

B: No.

A: What happens next?

B: One of us says, "We're almost there, we're almost there." After another hour, we arrive, and someone else says, "Here we are." He shines a flashlight on the walls of the cave; part of the wall is like giant man-size diamonds.

A: What color?

B: White with inclusions of gray and white, so maybe a dark white. I say, "Well, let's get started." We open our backpacks and take out tools, hammers, shovels and all kinds of chisels. We begin to chisel the walls to get the stones. We chisel and chisel and chisel... We see that there's something inside those stones. They are actually containers that will have to be opened later.

A: *What are they made of?*

B: Some type of diamond. There are six of us. We chisel out six containers of diamond. It takes a long time, and we chisel without breaks. We need to get them out of the walls. They're very heavy, so it takes a long time. We have ropes and stretchers, which we use to carry the containers as we head back. The way back is much harder because we have to carry very heavy things. We eventually reach the ladder and tap hard on it to signal that we've arrived. Ropes are lowered, and a few people come down to help us. Eventually we get the containers up.

A: *What are your thoughts about those containers?*

B: I know what's in the containers.

A: *What's in the containers?*

B: Our bodies are there.

A: *Your bodies?*

B: Yes. After we get all the containers out, we go up and into a tent to clean up. Then evening comes, and we decide to open the containers. Each of us works on a different one. It's a container, but it looks like a giant sealed stone, completely sealed. We start to carve the stone carefully to avoid harming whatever is inside. Eventually, I'm able to open the stone. I break enough pieces to get to what's inside, and I see myself there. It's my body, actually. I'm trying to remember how I got into a situation where I'm removing my own body out of the ground, out of this container, because I'm not dead, I'm alive.

A: *What do you remember?*

B: I remember something about parallel worlds, but I can't remember clearly... I'm beginning to remember that there was a collision between two planets, between our planet and another one. That collision was actually between two parallel universes with very similar frequencies, so they collided. There was a collision and during that collision, there was an overlap between the planets, and part of the other planet became our planet. It's as if the other planet took the place of ours. So all the people that were there, our counterparts, died, and their bodies materialized in our planet, buried deep underground in the place where the overlap occurred.

A: *Did everybody there die?*

B: All the people who were in the area that overlapped died.

A: *Didn't the entire planet overlap?*

B: No, not the entire planet, just some of it, like two balls that overlap only a small section.

A: *How did you know what happened?*

B: We had a few scientists who studied the event. They understood it and measured it.

A: *What caused that event?*

B: Nobody knows. Nobody knows why the frequencies became similar. Maybe there was some attraction between them, between the planets and the universes.

A: *How has that manifested physically in your planet when it happened? Did you feel it?*

B: No. We didn't feel it physically, but our scientists were able to measure it with their instruments. The instruments could measure the frequency of each area of this planet and were able to determine the places where the frequency was slightly different; where it happened. Every being here has a signature, like an aura, that can be measured and quantified. It's in the database of the population. They saw radiation of different auras coming from this place. That's how they knew whose counterpart had died.

A: *After they died, was there also radiation?*

B: The radiation remained even after they died. That's how the scientists knew where to find them and dig.

A: *How many were there? Were those the only ones that died from the parallel universe, or were there more?*

B: There were a lot more. I went there only with about six from my area.

A: *So you were specifically called to dig them?*

B: Yes.

A: *Why?*

B: Because there are too many, and it's impossible to hire contractors for that. Everyone is supposed to get his body out, and if he can't, he can hire someone else. Everyone prefers to dig himself out.

A: *Now that you're there looking at your body, how do you feel?*

B: It's a little weird to see myself dead. I wonder what his life was like, my life. Because it's me, I'm supposed to feel some strong emotion, but I don't feel anything special, even though it looks like me.

A: *What happens next? What's done with the bodies?*

B: They're taken to the lab to verify that it's really us, or our counterparts. It's been decided that because they died, we have to die too; otherwise there will be no balance. The scientists think that because my counterpart died in a parallel universe, I must die in this universe. Otherwise, there would be an imbalance that would create more collisions. It's as if something must be returned to the other universe to avoid another collision.

A: *So what happens?*

B: There's a general protest and unrest. "No way, it makes no sense. It's murder!" But the scientists are more powerful than anything. If they state something, then it's true. It's impossible to argue with them. The common good is more important.

A: *How do you feel about that?*

B: Not good. I don't want to die. I feel that it's enough that I already died in the parallel universe; I don't have to die again. But most of the population disagrees with that.

A: *Then what happens?*

B: They decide to kill us.

A: *How?*

B: With electricity. They think the electrical energy of our death will transfer our bodies to the parallel universe. They want to send us there dead.

A: *What do you do? Do you resist?*

B: We resist, but there's nothing we can do about it. They take us somewhere and give us sleeping pills.

A: *How many are you?*

B: Currently around twenty.

A: *Is that everyone?*

B: No, there are more, but the killing is done in batches. We take a sleeping pill... then they hook us up to electrodes and electrocute us.

A: *What happens after you leave your body?*

B: I see people bury my body wrapped in stone, deep in the ground.

A: *What happens next?*

B: Everything is repeated again. I see myself going to dig myself out of the ground...

A: *What do you think when you see that?*

B: I think it's sad that I'm stuck in an endless death.

A: *Is it repeated again and again?*

B: Yes.

A: *Now that you're out of your body, do you know what started it? Does it have a beginning?*

B: The first explosion, the collision.

A: *What caused the collision?*

B: Many people started thinking about the existence of a parallel planet, so they got close to it.

A: *Scientists or people in the population?*

B: It started with scientists, but somehow it spread to the rest of the population.

A: *So because they were aware of it and thought about it, it brought the planets closer?*

B: Yes.

A: *Did they think about it on the other planet?*

B: Yes.

A: *So at the same time, people on both planets began to think about it?*

B: Somehow one caused the other...

A: *Did it only happen on two planets or were there more?*

B: There were more, but these two, by chance, were very close, then it was as if "it's easier to exist at the same time."

A: *When they killed those people to balance the universe, were the bodies of those people really sent to the other planet?*

B: Yes.

A: *So who went to dig out the bodies, if those people were already dead?*

B: At the moment of the collision, the planet where the people died was actually restored. It's as if the collision was only the physical manifestation of the situation, but in reality nothing was destroyed. It's as if it was all recreated. It became an endless cycle, an endless cause and effect.

A: *So the people who seemed to have died and transferred to the other planet were actually recreated at that moment on the original planet?*

B: Yes.

A: *On the two planets, were there living people and bodies at the same time?*

B: Yes. There were two different universes and planets, and the same thing happened in both.

A: *Was it a time loop?*

B: Yes.

A: *What happens after you leave that body and understand what happened? Does it go on forever?*

B: Yes, but because there is an infinite number of things, it doesn't matter.

A: *If you're now outside of that body, is there another awareness, in the meantime, that's experiencing the same thing?*

B: If there are beings who want to experience it, then yes. It's like a vessel... A vessel was created to experience that.

A: *Is it like a story that exists and anyone who wants to experience it, can?*

B: Yes.

A: *Can you now leave it and move on?*

B: Yes.

A: May I speak with Ben's Mediator?

Mediator: Yes.

A: Why did you choose to show him that he died in a collision between two planets?

M: I wanted to let him know that everything happens in parallel, and that there's such a thing as collective thinking.

A: What do you mean by collective thinking?

M: If most conscious beings think about something, it can happen.

A: So when many people think the same thing, they make it happen?

M: Yes.

A: Why is it important for him to know that?

M: Because he doesn't believe it. It's hard for him to believe what he can't see.

A: In this story, is it significant that the scientists decided to kill those people? Is there anything that Ben's supposed to learn from that?

M: Yes, scientists don't know everything. They didn't have to kill them because nothing was really lost on that planet. What's perceived is not what really happens.

A: Does Ben think they do know everything?

M: No. But there's a lot more room for answers than he thinks. He knows they don't know everything, but they know even less than he thinks they do.

A: So they didn't have to kill those people?

M: No.

A: If they weren't killed, would this loop still have been created?

M: No.

A: Is there a message in this story?

M: Thoughts have to be used cautiously. When everyone had the same thought it caused a collision.

A: Do you mean thoughts about himself or in general?

M: Both.

A: In this case, was it thoughts or beliefs that caused the collision?

M: It was the certainty that a parallel universe existed.

A: Does a thought that lacks certainty also have the power to create things?

M: It does, but its power is minimal.

A: In order for a thought to have more power, one has to be sure, to know it?

M: Yes. There has to be constant awareness.

A: Is it true that we create our own reality through our collective thoughts?

M: It's not only us; it's the whole universe. The whole universe is one big thought.

A: If people on Earth begin to think more positively, will their life improve?

M: Yes.

COMMENTARY

Parallel universes exist and thoughts have power to affect events. Two planets in parallel universes collided because their existence became known. The event was misunderstood by scientists, and lives were unnecessarily lost.

MESSAGES

1. Collective thinking affects reality, so thinking has to be done cautiously.
2. What's perceived is not always what really happens.
3. Positive thinking will improve life.

STUDY QUESTIONS

1. Are you aware of the way you create your reality with your beliefs and thoughts?
2. What positive thoughts can you focus on in order to improve your life?

AFFIRMATIONS

1. I release to the world only kind and positive thoughts.
2. I contribute to the joy and happiness of humankind with my optimism and good intentions.

SESSION SEVENTEEN

A Planet of Crystals

THIS is another session we conducted without preparing questions ahead of time.

Ben: I see a very shiny planet. All of it is made of small crystals in bright colors, translucent and changing.

Anat: Where's the light coming from?

B: Apparently from inside the planet. There's no light from the outside.

A: Can't you see a sun or anything like it?

B: No.

A: Can you land on the planet?

B: I can't. I'd have to become part of the planet.

A: Then become part of the planet and tell me what happens.

B: I'm part of the planet now.

A: What does it feel like?

B: Energetic motion. I am the motion. I feel like a wave of energy. There are other waves next to me, and they're colliding with me. It hurts. It's not exactly painful, but uncomfortable, unnatural. I try to avoid the other waves, but not always successfully. Sometimes I'm able to merge with other waves, and then we move faster, but then when we collide, it's even more uncomfortable and unnatural. The only thing that happens is that we collide, stop, and move. I feel that we're part of something bigger, and this planet is a part of something else; I'm not sure what. I think we're part of a larger system of planets. We're the center of something. We're some type of consciousness, probably of a star system. When I move, I know that something is changing in this system.

A: Does your movement cause a change in the system?

B: Yes. I think it's a change in the movement of the other planets. When there are no collisions, there is harmony among the planets. We're inside crystals, and each time we collide, we change color and glow. There are dark places where there are no collisions, and places with more light that are stable, so the waves move fast without colliding. But in the end, there's always a collision somewhere.

A: *Expand your awareness to the larger system and describe it.*

B: There are planets that collide with one another and disappear. With every collision here, something happens outside. There are collisions of asteroids with one another and of planets. They occur because of the collisions in the crystal planet. Because I'm only one of these waves, I can't stop it. I have no control. I only have control of myself. No matter what I do, where I turn or how fast, it doesn't help. The collisions continue.

A: *Do you want to stop them?*

B: Yes. I feel that we must reach calm and harmony.

A: *Are others also trying?*

B: Yes, but there's no guidance, no master to direct it all.

A: *What happens next?*

B: I decide to go. I have to figure out where this master is. I return to where I came from, outside this planet. I decide to merge with what surrounds this planet.

A: *What surrounds the planet?*

B: Nothingness, like a void.

A: *Then what happens?*

B: Now I'm in this void. I feel in control, complete control.

A: *What do you control?*

B: Everything. I decide to organize the planet with the crystals. I make all the energies and waves move in the same direction, so that there are no collisions. All the planets are moving perfectly in circular motions. Everything is perfect.

A: *How do you feel?*

B: I don't feel anything. It's perfect.

A: *Then what happens?*

B: After a while, the waves become difficult to control because they are beginning to disperse.

A: *So what happens?*

B: I go back to the crystal planet and continue colliding. It's much easier.

A: *Why?*

B: Because I'm free. Even though it's not comfortable, it is freedom.

A: *Why is it freer now than before?*

B: Because I have to control only myself. I don't have to move in a certain direction and can move wherever I want.

A: *Is it freer than being in the void, being the master?*

B: Yes. Freer but... I don't know...

A: *Do you keep colliding?*

B: Yes, but then I decide to leave it again. I want to merge with the void again. I merge with the void around the planet. I'm trying to find a way to make it easy to control. I'm in control again, and I make everything move to the same place, so there is harmony. When it gets harder, I enlarge the planet.

A: *Then what happens?*

B: After I enlarge the planet, there's room for the waves to move more freely. They all move in the same direction and are easier to control. When I understand that, I decide to leave.

A: *How do you leave?*

B: I use willpower.

A: *What's happening after you leave? Is the system still moving in harmony?*

B: No, it isn't. Everything is glowing and changing colors. There is no harmony, no harmony at all. I see planets colliding and exploding. The entire space is full of collisions.

A: *What are your thoughts about it?*

B: Without me this place cannot exist. It will die. I feel a great responsibility, but there's nothing I can do.

A: *Do you leave anyway?*

B: Yes.

A: *How did the place exist before you arrived? Did it exist before you arrived?*

B: No. It was created when I arrived.

A: *What happens when you leave?*

B: It becomes chaotic. It looks like a galaxy where planets collide with each other, explode and then disappear. Eventually all the planets will disappear.

———⟨◇⟩———

A: *May I speak with Ben's Mediator?*

Mediator: Yes.

A: *Why did you show Ben the planet with crystals?*

M: To make him realize that he's just like that universe. The waves on the crystal planet represent his thoughts, his ego. The awareness above the thoughts is the void surrounding the planet. If he wants, he can control his thoughts. He just has to be above them, surround them and envelop them.

A: *In order to create harmony?*

M: Yes.

A: *In the example you showed him, what do the asteroids and planets signify?*

M: All that he thinks is going on outside, the entire external world. When there are collisions, the outside world collapses because it's not in harmony.

A: *Do you mean that when his thoughts are not in harmony, they affect the external world negatively?*

M: Yes.

A: *When he was in the crystals, one wave of energy, he could only control himself and not others. What does that symbolize?*

M: His thoughts have lives of their own and are not synchronized. As long as they're not under control, they go where they want. Sometimes they're good thoughts, but usually there are collisions that cause collapses.

A: *In order to control the waves of energy he had to go out to the void. Does that mean that he should get out and be above his thoughts?*

M: Yes.

A: *When he went to the void, he felt that he could control every-thing. Does that mean that if he reaches that situation, he will be able to control all thoughts?*

M: Yes, but it's hard.

A: *He said that after a while it gets hard. Why?*

M: Thoughts have energy, and there is friction between them. The situation inside the planet, the brain, is not static, but dynamic. If one doesn't pay attention, thoughts move and collide again. One needs to pay attention very carefully. Be like a watchdog all the time.

A: *In this example he found a solution. He enlarged the planet, and that made the waves easier to control. What does that mean?*

M: It means that increasing the number of things you think about makes control easier.

A: *Do you mean expanding one's world view?*

M: Yes, but not necessarily in the holistic sense, even in small things.

A: *Can you give an example?*

M: Anything you can think of. If you add things to think about, you can facilitate this harmony.

A: *After he tried to be the master and saw how difficult it was, he returned being an energy wave in the planet. He felt free, and it was easier for him. What does that signify?*

M: It's easy to think a single thought. It's easy to say the same thing all the time, but it's difficult to control thoughts.

A: *After he enlarged the planet, it was easier to create harmony. He said that after he understood that, he decided to leave. What is the meaning of that?*

M: It means that he understood what to do. That was enough.

A: *Why did he feel guilty when he decided to leave?*

M: Because he knew that if he had stayed longer, the entire system would have lived longer; but he only used it to understand things.

A: *Was that experience real or only a metaphor?*

M: It was real.

A: *So it's a real experience that's also a metaphor about how a human functions?*

M: Yes.

A: *Here's a question that may be related. Can you explain what the ego is?*

M: The ego is thoughts that are out of control, everything that is under the general awareness.

A: *So, when thoughts are under control, they're no longer ego?*

M: Correct.

A: *And how would someone who reaches that situation of being in control feel? What would his life look like?*

M: He would be in harmony with everything. Nothing would hurt him.

A: *What is that awareness that's supposed to control thoughts, if it's not the thoughts themselves?*

M: Just awareness.

A: *Is it separate from thoughts?*

M: Yes, but it's usually absorbed in thoughts.

A: *The same way Ben was absorbed by the planet of crystals?*

M: Yes. This awareness should want to wake up in order to be present.

A: *As he decided to leave the planet and look for the master?*

M: Yes, but he was not the master. He became the master, but with humans it's different.

A: *How is it different?*

M: The awareness and the thoughts are separate.

A: *But most people don't know that or don't even notice?*

M: Right.

A: *So we have to understand that thoughts are a separate thing and they can be controlled?*

M: They can be observed from the outside and controlled.

A: *Does it take work?*

M: It takes constant work when you want to do it. At any moment you can do it.

COMMENTARY

In this session, a planet is used to demonstrate how humans function. It is a real experience that also serves as a metaphor. Thoughts have lives of their own, and if they are not under control, the external world collapses. It is possible to control thoughts and thus create a harmonious life.

MESSAGES

1. To control thoughts, one has to be above them, surround them and envelop them.
2. When thoughts are not synchronized, the external world reflects that.
3. Awareness and thoughts are separate.

STUDY QUESTIONS

1. Are you able to distinguish between your awareness and your thoughts?
2. Are you aware of how events in your life are affected by the quality of your thoughts?

AFFIRMATIONS

1. I am connecting with my infinite awareness; therefore I have more and more control over my thoughts.
2. I create harmony in my life by taking charge of my thoughts.

SESSION EIGHTEEN

Nothing to Fear, Nothing to Worry About

Before we started the following session, I thought to myself that I wanted to hear more about the colorful planet, but I didn't mention it to Ben. Again, he had no questions.

Ben: I'm on the colorful planet. I want to leave and go to a place where there's no fear.

Anat: Is there fear on the colorful planet?

B: No, but I want to go to a place where all the emotions, except fear, are present. I want to see what it's like.

A: Is there such a place? Have you heard of a place like that?

B: Yes. It's like Earth, but people are not afraid and have no worries.

A: So what happens?

B: I leave the colorful planet. I'm moving in space and see the planet I want to go to. It's blue and pink. I'm getting closer, approaching it. I arrive at a village with people.

A: What do they look like?

B: Similar to humans, but squarer and less round. It's as if they're made of boxes, but not exactly. I see that everyone seems happy. I want to be born there. I return to the colorful planet, merge with it and die there.

A: What happens after you die on the colorful planet?

B: I find myself in a forest. I'm a kid, about eleven years old. It's dark, and no one is there. I'm not worried or afraid. I have a desire to find out where I am, but it doesn't bother me. I keep walking in the woods, and apparently it's night because it seems like it's going to be dawn soon. The sun is starting to rise. I manage to get out of the woods. I see my house, approach it and then open the door. I see my father sitting there. He says to me, "There you are. Where have you been?"

I tell him, "I got lost in the woods." He says: "But you know I told you not to go into the forest after dark because there are all kinds of creatures that can kill you." I reply, "Yes, I know, I didn't realize it got dark. I intended to come out while it was still light, but it got dark, and I didn't notice, so I got lost." He says, "Well, all right."

I ask my dad, "Why didn't you come to find me?" He replies, "I knew you would be all right, and nothing would happen to you. It was only a matter of time until you got home." I ask, "But didn't you worry? Weren't you afraid that something would happen to me, that I might get killed by those creatures in the forest?"

He answers, "No. Until about age fifteen or sixteen people worry, but later they don't. When we reach a certain age, we don't worry, and we're not afraid." I ask, "So I, too, won't be afraid anymore and stop worrying?" He answers, "Yes. Everyone who lives here reaches an age when there's awareness or understanding that there's nothing to fear and nothing to worry about."

I say, "I want to get to that state. But maybe I'd reached it already because I was walking in the forest and was not worried. I knew I would make it." My father replies: "Yes, it starts at the age of ten or eleven when children worry less; but when you reach the age of fifteen, sixteen, or seventeen, you don't worry anymore."

A: Move forward in time to a significant event in that life.

B: Now I'm fifteen. I'm supposed to start a new grade at school the next day, and I'm worried. What's going to happen? Am I going to fit in? It really bothers me so I go to my father and ask him, "Dad, why am I so worried and afraid?" He says to me, "Don't worry. You won't worry, you won't be afraid." I believe him because I see that he's not afraid; but I myself, am afraid. I go to sleep. I wake up in the morning and I'm still scared. I go to school and see other children my age and other ages.

Then someone older shows up and says, "If this is your first day, you should follow me." I follow him, and I see a group of fifteen or twenty others that go with him. We follow him, and then he opens a door in a corridor with many doors. He tells each one of us to go through a different door. I enter the room and see a desk with a chair next to it. On the desk there are glasses with strange wires attached to them. I hear a voice in the background telling me to sit down and put the glasses on. I do as I'm told. When I wear the glasses, I begin to see all kinds of shapes slowly forming in the darkness, and they become clear. I see shapes that look like lightning bolts, or one strong lightning from which other bolts are extending toward the ground. There is no ground, but they're moving downward. I see that one of these lightning bolts responds to me. I understand that it represents me and my thoughts. I hear a voice saying that the goal is to make me not worry anymore. I don't understand why I shouldn't worry anymore. Then, the voice tells me that the lightning that responded to me, really represents me. The rest represent the other children. We're now connected through the glasses in the rooms.

The voice says that when I stop bothering myself with what others think, I won't worry anymore. I begin to see all kinds of movies about myself. They show me that every time I worried, it was because I cared about what others thought. What causes fear is actually only an illusion. I'm my own master, and I can control what I receive and what I block. The voice tells me that the most important thing I can do for myself, that affects me the most, is to take care of my own thoughts and not worry about what other people think.

After about two hours of explanations of the various scenes of my life and of these lightning bolts, which are actually all thoughts of the other children, I begin to understand that there's really nothing to fear anymore and nothing to worry about. There's an infinite acceptance.

Suddenly, everything shuts down, so I take my glasses off, leave the room, and I don't worry anymore. I meet the other kids, and I'm not afraid to talk to them. No one is afraid to talk to each other because nobody cares what others think of him or her. Everyone is much more open and genuine. There's harmony amongst everyone. I tell myself that I can't believe I was afraid and worried all those years, about nothing, nothing. I was afraid of illusions. When this day is over I go back home. I tell my dad I don't understand what I was worried about all those years, and why I was afraid of the children. I was always so afraid of new things, how can that be? He tells me that's how it is here. When you reach the age of fifteen or sixteen, they show you that there's nothing to fear or worry about. The secret is that once you don't care what others think, you don't worry anymore.

A: *What happens next?*

B: Now I'm fifty or so and I have a child. I still live near the forest, but I'm not worried about my child. I'm trying to figure out why I'm not worried even though something might happen to him. He might get killed? Somehow this awareness that I don't care what others think causes me not to worry. It makes me think that everything will be fine. It makes me trust the universe to take care of the child. So I decide to leave.

A: *What do you mean?*

B: Leave this life.

A: *Why did you decide to leave?*

B: Because I learned what I needed to learn.

A: *Are you aware of that?*

B: Yes. Some part of me is.

A: *So what happens?*

B: I am reborn in the colorful planet. I just roam around and pass this information to others.

A: *What do you tell them?*

B: That there is a planet where people do not worry, and they feel everything except fear.

A: *Do you explain to them why it's like that?*

B: No. If I explain that, they won't go there because they'll know.

A: *So, what do they say when you tell them about it?*

B: That they want to try it. It sounds interesting to them.

A: *What do you think about that experience now that you're on the colorful planet?*

B: It can be implemented on any planet where there are worries.

A: *Do you know how to implement it on other planets?*

B: I don't exactly know how, but I know that if we don't care what others think, we don't worry.

A: *Even about things unrelated to others?*

B: Yes.

A: *Why is that?*

B: Because most concerns are about what others think, about how we look, how we think we look.

A: *Do you decide to do anything with this information now that you're on the colorful planet?*

B: I decide to try to remember it in the future.

A: *On other planets?*

B: Yes.

A: *Do you have a way to remember that?*

B: Not directly. When I get to other planets, I'll try to connect to this information somehow. Then maybe I'll be able to remember it, but it's hard.

A: *Why is it hard?*

B: Because every planet has to teach something, and we have to arrive as a blank slate.

A: *But do we still remember a little?*

B: It's possible to try to remember and to connect to the information. It's not exactly remembering; it's more like connecting to the information.

A: *Now that you're on the colorful planet, do you remember all your experiences from other planets?*

B: Yes.

A: *So every time you are on the colorful planet you remember everything?*

B: Yes.

A: *When you are on the colorful planet, are you more in touch with your Mediator?*

B: Yes.

A: *Can you talk to your Mediator, or are you the Mediator?*

B: The planet is the Mediator.

A: *Can you talk to the planet?*

B: Yes.

A: *Can you ask questions? Do you sometimes ask the planet questions?*

B: No. No, I ask questions of other entities.

A: *Only other entities?*

B: Yes, interaction is only with other entities. The entities are the same as the planet.

A: *Do you only remember your own experiences while you are on the colorful planet?*

B: Yes.

A: *Is there time on the colorful planet?*

B: No.

A: *Is there order to the experiences?*

B: Yes.

A: *Experiences happen one after another?*

B: There are experiences that have not occurred yet. In terms of my being, they have not occurred yet, but to another entity, they have already happened.

A: *Isn't it the same as time, if one thing happens after another?*

B: You can call it time, but it's more sequence than time.

A: *Is there an end to these experiences?*

B: No.

A: *Do they go on forever?*

B: Yes.

A: *Does a situation ever occur where you've already learned everything you needed to learn and experienced everything?*

B: No.

A: *Is there always more to experience?*

B: Yes.

A: *Is the colorful planet a physical place or is it more symbolic?*

B: It's the same thing. All is one consciousness.

A: *So it's not more or less physical than Earth?*

B: No.

———————⋖◇⋗———————

A: *Now that you're on the colorful planet, may I speak with Ben's Mediator?*

Mediator: Yes.

A: Why did you choose to show Ben the planet where there are no worries?

M: To show him that it's possible not to worry.

A: He currently doesn't think it's possible?

M: He thinks it's possible in theory, but he wants to put it into practice.

A: How can it be done?

M: You have to be aware all the time. Aware that what others think doesn't affect you. It's their business. Everyone has his role in the world. Each person is responsible for his or her own thoughts. You have to think about it all the time, all the time, all the time, and imagine it.

A: Ben described the experience of being shown those images with lightning bolts. Can something similar to that method be created on Earth?

M: You can create something like that, but you'll have to wear it all the time.

A: Why did it work there after only one time and here, we would need it all the time?

M: Because there they were kids, and it was easy to convince them. On Earth, people constantly think thoughts that are contrary to what they're shown. So you can't show it to them only once.

A: On that planet, did they not have contrary thoughts?

M: They were more innocent. They were children.

A: So if we start to teach children here, will it help? Is it easier to learn it at a young age?

M: It's easier, but you can't do it in a couple of hours.

A: But it was possible there?

M: Yes.

A: Why is it difficult to do on Earth?

M: It is hard to maintain the awareness that whatever others think of you is not important when all kinds of thoughts are running in your head. You have to get used to thinking about it, and it might become easier. It should be in the background all the time. Maybe someday it will become second nature, but most of your life you have to remember it and remember the pictures.

A: What pictures?

M: The pictures I projected one by one like a movie.

A: When Ben saw that they were only characters?

M: Yes.

A: If one doesn't care what others think, can you explain how it helps with other things? For example, in his case, something might have happened to his child. How does it help in that case? Because it's seemingly unrelated to what others think.

M: There is more confidence. When you don't care what others think, it inspires some type of trust, a sense of security. It's not just self-confidence; born from it is an existential trust. So, there's a feeling that everything will be fine. It's what comes of it. There's no direct link, but an existential trust in the universe is born from it.

A: So according to what you say, our biggest obstacle is that we care about what others think?

M: We care, and we're afraid of what other people think of us.

A: So the moment we stop caring about what people think, everything will be easier?

M: Everything will be much easier. It doesn't mean we should be inconsiderate of other people, but it shouldn't be an obstacle to our self-worth. We can be considerate of the desires and thoughts of others, knowing that they can't hurt us. This world of thoughts, of consciousness, is us; we are an entire world, and from the outside that world cannot be hurt. We just have to remember that.

A: What about the fear of physical pain, for example?

M: This existential sense of security inspires trust that there won't be physical pain, and that if there is physical pain, it won't be strong. So there's nothing to worry about.

A: I talked to Ben about my difficulty to implement spiritual understandings in everyday life. It's hard not to worry; it's hard not to be afraid.

M: You should try to connect to the awareness more rather than to the thoughts. Then it will be easier to implement things you know.

A: How can I connect to it more?

M: Be the awareness. Be aware of the thoughts from the outside. Being aware is just being aware; there is no action. It just happens. If you are aware, it happens.

A: Does it also require practice or effort?

M: It requires effort at first, but then it gets easier.

COMMENTARY

The subject in this session is fear. It presents the idea that when we don't care what other people think about us, there is no fear. When we are secure to the point where we are not occupied with what others think of us, we have an existential trust in the universe.

MESSAGES

1. Fear is caused by the illusion that what others think of you is important.
2. Once you don't care what others think, you don't worry anymore.
3. You are your own master, and you can control what you receive and what you block.

STUDY QUESTIONS

1. How often do you allow yourself to be influenced by what others think of you?
2. How would your life be different if you truly did not care about others' opinions of you?

AFFIRMATIONS

1. I am the master of my own life, and I make my decisions based on my own judgment and intuition.
2. I trust myself to do my best in every situation; therefore I feel safe and secure at all times.

SESSION NINTEEN

The Courage to Want

PRIOR to conducting this session, Ben said that he still felt unhappy and would like to enjoy life more.

Ben: I see sand. I'm a man. I'm wearing shoes made of wood and leather. I'm dressed in rags and walking on the sand.

Anat: Is there anyone else there?

B: No.

A: How do you feel?

B: I don't feel anything special.

A: Is it day or night?

B: There is light; I guess it is day.

A: What else do you see around you?

B: A plain and some hills. There are more hills out in the distance.

A: How is the weather?

B: Pleasant.

A: Are you carrying anything?

B: Water in a leather canteen.

A: Keep walking until you get where you're going, or until something happens.

B: I'm walking, and I see a hole in the ground. I know I need to climb down the hole. I go in and sink slowly. I don't see the bottom. It's unclear how deep it is. I'm sinking slowly at first; then I start picking up speed. I seem to fall into the ground, or whatever it is, sand. I'm falling quickly.

A: What happens next?

B: I'm still falling. Suddenly I feel a thump on my feet. I think I'm lying on a rock. I see currents of orange fluids, like lava. I get up and start walking. The ground is mostly rocky, but some of it is lava that I'm careful not to touch.

A: *Are you underground?*

B: Yes, I think so.

A: *Is there light?*

B: There is no light, but I can see because of the lava. The place is familiar to me; I've been here before. It seems so familiar.

A: *Do you know where you're going?*

B: I think so. I'm walking, and it seems I'm going further down. Occasionally there is a step, so I'm going down deeper. The air is hot, but not too bad. I'm walking, and far away I see several people dressed in rags.

A: *What are they doing?*

B: Nothing, they are sitting. I'm approaching them. I reach them and they're all looking at me expectantly.

A: *What are you doing?*

B: I have bread in my bag. I give it to them. They take it and start eating savagely.

A: *Are you eating too?*

B: No, I'm not hungry.

A: *What do you think when you look at them?*

B: I see that everyone resembles me. All of them resemble me, and I feel good that they are eating.

A: *What happens next?*

B: I tell them that soon I have to leave. One of them says to me: "No, stay here with us." I say: "No, I have to go. I can't stay here. It's like a dead end; there is nothing to do here." Another says to me: "Don't go. What are we going to do? What will we eat? How will we survive?" I reply: "I will come again and bring you food." They look at me with such sad eyes, understanding eyes. They understand that I can't stay there.

I say: "Maybe you will come with me? You don't have to stay here." Then one of them says: "No, we can't go with you." I say: "I know, but perhaps we will try anyway? It will be good for you; there are many things out there that you don't have here. You don't have to be hungry all the time; you could be outside and eat as much as you want." They begin to be afraid and someone starts crying that he doesn't want to go. I understand why he is crying and scared. They are all too scared, so I'm not trying to convince them. I'm sorry they are not coming, but on the other hand, part of me is pleased that I won't have to take care of them on the way out.

A: *How do you feel about the outside?*

B: I want to go outside.

A: *So what are you doing?*

B: I empty the bag. I also have water there. I give it to them and say that I have to go. I take just a little water, whatever I have left in the canteen. I get up and start walking. I'm not going the way I came from; I'm walking in a different direction. I'm still walking underground, and I start to climb stairs. Occasionally there is a step up. Suddenly I see this wall of sand; sand that flows upward. I get close to the wall and touch it, insert my hand and feel a pull upward, as if the sand wants to pull me up. I insert my entire arm, my shoulder, part of my body and at the end all of me. I'm being pulled upward and picking up speed. When I go up I feel I'm merging with the sand and becoming sand. I am sand and somehow I'm leaving the ground that is also filled with sand and I am part of it. I'm flying high up as sand.

A: *What does it feel like?*

B: I only feel an upward movement. That's all I am, one big movement.

A: *Any thoughts?*

B: No. I continue flying, and then I feel that I'm approaching the ground again, but it's not the same ground I came from. This is another ground, another place. I am still sand and there is sand in this ground. I collide with the ground and get sucked into the sand. I am still sand, but slowly I'm morphing into a unique form. I become something separate from the sand. Suddenly I find myself again on the... again, a thump on a rock. It seems I fainted or something. Then I wake up, and beside me there are several other figures that are similar to me. They are wearing rags.

A: *Human beings?*

B: I don't know if human beings... living beings in rags. They don't talk to each other. I know I'm there forever, for life. I'm hungry and thirsty. I have nothing to do. We wonder around there all day doing nothing.

A: Is there nothing to eat or drink?

B: No.

A: So what happens?

B: Nothing, we don't do anything, just sit and walk occasionally.

A: What does that place look like?

B: Gray with lava pools.

A: How long are you there?

B: I don't know, seems like a long time.

A: Move forward in time until something happens.

B: One day I die. I somehow accidentally slip and fall into one of the lava pools. It's impossible to survive that.

A: What happens after you die?

B: I'm out of my body. I'm still underground, so I'm trying to get out. I'm able to climb up through the rocks and sand. I'm walking away and see a planet. From afar the planet seems orange-yellow. As I move away I see that it's actually two planets that look the same and are relatively close to each other, compared to the other planets there. I get farther and farther away from the planets. Then I see that the planets are in fact parts of the universe, of my own brain. I see that I'm not dead really, I just woke up. I just woke up and all I did was... I was just a thought. I was a consciousness in my own universe. I realize that all the people I saw underground were my desires, my wants. Only occasionally I went to visit them, give them food. They didn't want to get out and I didn't force them to leave, but I could have forced them out. I didn't do it, so they stayed underground hungry. I could have gotten them out when I was on the first planet, but on the second one I couldn't have. I was buried and nobody could get me out, the same way that no one could get out the other characters. In both cases no one got out; in both cases we chose to stay inside. So I understand that there is a choice, there is always a choice. But on the second planet I couldn't leave.

A: Why? Why was it different?

B: No one came to show us the way, and we didn't look for it by ourselves. But even when they showed us the way... When I showed them the way on the first planet, they didn't want to leave anyway. So what does it matter if it's possible to get out or not? In any case they did not get out. So what does it matter if the door is open or not? Probably, if I had insisted enough, I would have gotten them out from the first place. I did not insist...

A: *But you yourself got out?*

B: Yes, I came from the outside already, so part of me was outside, but other parts were inside.

A: *So you didn't insist on getting all the parts out?*

B: No.

A: *Do you now think that you should have insisted?*

B: Yes.

A: *Is there anything else you learned from this experience?*

B: That there are situations you can change and others you can't. It may seem that you can never change a situation, but that's not true. Sometimes it is possible, and there is a way out even if you're too afraid to look for it. It's just a matter of choice.

A: *May I speak with Ben's Mediator?*

Mediator: Yes.

A: *You showed Ben a situation where he was underground, and he explained that the beings there were his wishes, his wants. Why did you choose to show him that?*

M: I wanted him to understand that every time he wants something and doesn't do out of fear, something inside of him dies.

A: *Are there many things he wants and doesn't do out of fear?*

M: Yes, he keeps holding himself back, out of fear and out of shyness.

A: *Does Ben know when this is happening? Is he aware that there are things he wants and doesn't do?*

M: Not always. Sometimes he makes up reasons ahead of time for not wanting things.

A: *So he wouldn't have to even deal with it?*

M: Yes.

A: *Is he aware of doing that?*

M: Not always.

A: *What would help him be more aware and not do it?*

M: He should think thoroughly to determine whether he wants something or not, even if he thinks he doesn't.

A: *Is that one of the reasons it is difficult for him to enjoy life?*

M: Yes. He is afraid to want to do things he can enjoy because it sometimes involves meeting new people. It's something he's trying to avoid, so he is afraid to test things he could want and enjoy. He leaves his desires buried, even when he doesn't know what they are.

A: *Are most of his fears related to fear of other people?*

M: Not exactly fear of others, more fear of the unknown. If he gets over it, he will be able to find more things he likes to do. He will be able to enjoy his life more.

A: *What would be a good way to start?*

M: Look for things to do and just do them. Take the plunge.

A: *It doesn't matter so much what?*

M: Not anything, mainly things that have potential.

A: *Will he know what has potential?*

M: Yes.

A: *So Ben has the potential to enjoy life much more?*

M: Yes.

A: *Well, that is good news... So it's not that complicated to enjoy life?*

M: No.

A: *The thing that is stopping him is fear?*

M: All of us.

A: *Are we all held back by fear?*

M: Fear, lack of faith that we can have fun, and thinking we know what we would enjoy and what not.

A: *So we dismiss things that way?*

M: Yes.

A: *To have more fun, is it better to try things anyway and not to dismiss them?*

M: Yes.

COMMENTARY

This session is an illustration of what happens when we give in to fear and hold ourselves back. When we have desires or wants that we ignore, parts of us die. There is internal suffering and hopelessness. It is possible to enjoy life and experience joy when we are more in touch with our desires and take action to meet our needs.

MESSAGES

1. Every time you give in to fear and hold back, part of you dies.
2. Do not dismiss things that have potential for enjoyment until you try them.

STUDY QUESTIONS

1. Are you aware of things you might be afraid to want?
2. What can you think of that may have potential to increase enjoyment in your life?

AFFIRMATIONS

1. I am in touch with my inner desires and am confident in my ability to meet my needs.
2. I deserve to be happy and enjoy life, so I feel joy when trying new things.

SESSION TWENTY

A House Made of Lights

THIS is the last session we had before Ben returned to Israel. He had no questions.

Ben: I see a white surface. I don't think I have a body. I'm moving, and I see all kinds of lights in different colors in the distance. I'm moving in that direction. I see groups of lights. They're beautiful. I don't know what is creating the lights, but I see that the lights are creating all sorts of things. Now they're creating a house.

Anat: What is the house made of?

B: At first it is made of lights, but gradually it becomes like a normal house. I continue moving forward. I see another group of lights creating a tree. The lights are creating everything I know. They are creating a car... I continue, and I see many more groups of lights. There are also lights that create rain, drops of water, dogs... I continue moving... I see a cage. Inside the cage I see my form.

A: What does your form look like?

B: It is full of bright colored lights, all colors. It looks human, a man. It is an outline of a person, me. I know it's me, my form, or a part of me. I'm trying to figure out what this form is doing here. It has no face, but it seems like it is looking at me. I move around the cage, and it keeps turning toward me, not moving, but somehow always turning toward me, looking at me. I want to talk to this form. I think it is beginning to talk to me. It says it is my ego. I ask it: "Why are you here?" The figure tells me that I have created it like I created the rest of the things here. I ask: "Why did I create you?" He says I created him in order to protect myself. "Why do I need protection?" He says I need protection from the world, whatever happens in the world, on Earth. I ask: "Why do I need this figure to protect me? Why can't I protect myself?" He tells me I need something tangible to protect me, something to react quickly and physically because I am not physical and cannot defend myself against physical things, or what I perceive as physical.

I ask the figure if he is also responsible for my fears. He tells me he is. I ask: "Why are you in a cage?" He tells me I put him in a cage, so he would not escape. I ask: "Why would you escape? Why am I afraid that you would escape?" He says that I feel like I need him, but I know I don't. Without the cage he would escape. I ask: "What do you mean when you say: I feel like I need you, but I know I don't?" I feel like I need him because he is there. He makes sure that I feel like I need him, but I know I don't. I know he was created only to get me going in life, and he is not needed anymore.

A: What happens next?

B: I continue moving. I see all white. There are lights, and new things are constantly created. I only see white and lights. I keep moving in this white. I see black in the distance. I'm getting closer to this black... Now everything is black. I think it's... as if things are being destroyed... as if I'm in a situation in which whatever was created by the lights before, is collapsing. I'm in a constant state of things that are ceasing to be. And it's all black.

A: Is there a feeling?

B: It's a state of being; it's not a feeling. As if every time I cease to be something else.

A: Like what?

B: Everything. Houses, trees, plants...

A: How do they cease to be? Do they disappear?

B: Yes, but it's like I'm disappearing. I want to get out of this state.

A: So move forward in time until it's over, and you are out of it.

B: Now I'm back at the white.

A: What do you see there?

B: Again things are constantly created.

A: Do you see your form there?

B: No.

A: Do you see the lights that are creating things?

B: Yes, the lights are creating things. I notice that I am also lights. I am all the colors together. I am like the form I've seen but much brighter.

A: *Do these lights have some form, outlines?*

B: No. The shape keeps changing.

A: *Move forward in time until something else happens, or until you are not there anymore.*

B: I'm in space. I see stars. I'm moving between the stars. I go back to the cloud.

A: *May I speak with Ben's Mediator?*

Mediator: Yes.

A: *Why did you show him the white surface with the lights that created all sorts of things?*

M: To make him realize that everything is created from the same place. All that he experiences, all that he sees, everything comes from the same place, from the place that he also comes from.

A: *What is that place?*

M: Overall awareness.

A: *Why is it important for him to see that everything comes from the same place?*

M: So that he would not feel alone and know that he is part of the universe, that everything is the same thing.

A: *You showed him his ego in a cage. What does that mean?*

M: He should know that he created the ego, that the ego was created for him. He created the cage, and if he wants, he can also destroy the cage and release the ego.

A: *And then what will happen?*

M: Then most likely a new ego will be created in a new cage.

A: *Why?*

M: To help him cope with the world.

A: *Does that mean that an ego is necessary?*

M: No, but it's the easiest way to deal with the world. If he accepts everything and knows that there are no such things as troubles and problems, he would not need the ego. But the world seems like there are such things, and that the ego is needed.

A: So as long as he believes there are troubles and problems, he needs the ego to deal with them?

M: Yes.

A: What can help him understand that there are no troubles and problems?

M: To remember where he came from. Remember the awareness.

A: How is that related to the colorful planet?

M: The colorful planet is part of the awareness; it is a product of it.

A: Was the colorful planet also created by the lights?

M: No. Everything experienced from the colorful planet, all the worlds that the beings experience, all are created by the lights. The colorful planet is part of the general awareness. The purpose of the lights is to create the physical experience.

A: At one point he said that he was also the lights, so does he also create this experience? Is that what it means?

M: When he becomes a physical being, he is created by the lights.

A: You said that if he understands that there are no troubles and problems, he will not need the ego. When he understands that, will the ego disappear?

M: It will be gone, but it'll be back later because this understanding is very difficult to maintain.

A: Is it possible to understand it permanently?

M: Yes, but then he will cease to be human. He will reach the Truth, and his experience on Earth will end.

A: Is it necessary to reach that understanding in order to end the experience on Earth?

M: Yes, to end it for good. When that happens, it is still possible to experience other things, but not on Earth.

A: Does that mean that as long as people, or entities, do not realize that, they will continue to return to Earth?

M: They will continue to return, not necessarily to Earth, perhaps to other places with the same principles.

A: Is learning that one of the objectives of these experiences?

M: Yes.

A: *So what happens after you learn that and finish with Earth?*

M: You go to places where you apply the understanding, begin to create things and not just understand that it is possible to create.

A: *What do you mean by creating things? We also create things on Earth. Do you mean creating things the same way the lights did?*

M: Yes.

A: *Is there some kind of scale of understanding or evolution on which we are progressing?*

M: You could say that.

A: *Then you showed him another place where everything was black, and things were destroyed. He said that he was in a state of things that were ceasing to be. Why did you show him that?*

M: To see the other side of creation, the destruction side. He should know that all the time things are either being created or destroyed, there is no in-between. He has to choose where to be, either creating or destroying. If he destroys, he is being destroyed; if he creates, he is being created.

A: *Can you give an example from his life of things he destroys?*

M: Negative thoughts destroy the body. Positive thoughts create options for more positive thoughts.

A: *Before the session Ben said he felt uneasy about the future, he doesn't know what will happen. Are the things you showed him related to that?*

M: If he tries to free his ego, he will feel better.

A: *But you said that if he releases it, there will be a new ego. Would it be an improvement?*

M: Yes. All is a matter of how much ego.

A: *How can he release the ego?*

M: Remember where he came from.

A: *The lights or the colorful planet?*

M: Everything.

A: *Will it help him be happier?*

M: Yes, if he remembers.

A: *He is going back to Israel soon. Can you give him some advice, guidance, about that?*

M: To remember where he came from and see things the way they really are: light.

COMMENTARY

All things come from the same place, from overall awareness. Everything is connected, and we're all part of the universe. But as long as we believe that there are such things as troubles and problems, we will be afraid and think that an ego is needed for protection.

MESSAGES

1. Remembering where we came from helps us to realize that there are no such things as troubles and problems.
2. There is a scale of understanding or evolution on which humans are progressing, until there is no need to experience places like Earth anymore.
3. All the time things are either being created or destroyed, there is no in-between.
4. Negative thoughts destroy the body. Positive thoughts create options for more positive thoughts.

STUDY QUESTIONS

1. What beliefs prevent you from releasing your ego?
2. Are you aware of the effects of your thoughts on your body?

AFFIRMATIONS

1. I feel more and more connected to everything, so I accept whatever occurs in my life with calmness and ease.
2. Through the power of my mind and my creative activities, I experience every moment to the fullest.

SESSION TWENTY-ONE

A Cockroach with Hands

WE had the following session in Israel during my short visit there. Ben wanted to feel more positive about his life.

Ben: I am a cockroach. I see cockroaches around.
Anat: What does it feel like to be a bug?
B: There is no feeling.
A: What are you focusing on now?
B: I see that I have hands. I'm looking at my hands. I don't understand how I have hands if I'm a cockroach.
A: What do your hands look like?
B: Normal.
A: Human hands?
B: Yes.
A: The other roaches around, do they also have hands?
B: No.
A: What size are your hands?
B: I don't know. Ordinary hands. I don't know what size I am.
A: Are you on the ground?
B: I'm on the grass outdoors. I'm looking at my hands. All the other bugs are busy looking for food. I don't know what I am actually. Am I a man? A cockroach? It's not making sense. What am I doing here? What does all this mean? I don't understand.
A: Do you remember how you got there?
B: I think I was brought here. I think I was brought here on a spacecraft.
A: Move back in time to when you're in the spaceship. Tell me what you look like on the spaceship.
B: I'm in a cage inside the spaceship.

A: Look at your hands. Do you have hands?

B: Yes.

A: Are you alone in the cage?

B: Yes.

A: Do you see other bugs there?

B: I'm not a cockroach on the spaceship.

A: What do you look like on the spaceship?

B: I have hands. I'm not a man; I'm a being. I have a long pointy head. It's green with spots. I have no nose. I have eyes, sort of a mouth and a long thin neck. I'm in a cage. Outside the cage there are other people, creatures; I don't know what they are, same as me. Each has a different shade. There are also shades of orange, not just green.

A: Do you communicate?

B: Not right now although I think I understand them.

A: What does it feel like to be there in the cage?

B: Scary. I don't know what's going to happen. I think I'm being punished for something.

A: Did you do something wrong?

B: I don't know. Apparently, I did something that made them put me in a cage.

A: Move back in time to find out how you got there.

B: I'm in a spacecraft. I operate all kinds of instruments.

A: What do you look like?

B: Same as before.

A: A green creature?

B: Yes. I tell the commander that I'm not happy. I'm not happy with myself, who I am, what I do. I'm very angry. He lets me know that if I'm not happy, he will make me happy. He is sending me to a cage.

A: Are you going to the cage on your own?

B: No. Others come and take me. I don't understand why he puts me in a cage.

A: Are you complaining? What are you saying?

B: Nothing. I'm not saying anything.

A: Move forward in time until you are taken out of the cage.

B: They are taking me out of the cage and down a long hallway. There are windows on both sides of the hallway. Every window has a different creature in it, creatures that look like cockroaches. They force me to look at them as we go, look at all the windows. It's scary. I don't know what's going to happen. I don't know why they want to show me those things. They are taking me, and I'm watching. We arrive at a door. They open it and inside there is a chair. They make me sit on the chair and tie my hands and feet, my body, to the chair, even my head. They put a mask on me with all kinds of wires. I don't know what it is. I'm very uncomfortable. They start to push all kinds of buttons and touch things. There is a shrill noise, a very high frequency noise. It gets unbearably noisy. I feel my body starting to change. I'm slowly becoming similar to one of the creatures seen in the windows.

A: *Are you still aware of what's happening?*

B: I'm still aware of myself, but my body is changing. At the end of this process, they take me and put me in another cage. After a long time, I don't know how long exactly, the commander comes and looks at me. He says: "I hope you're happy now." I don't respond. I'm very unhappy. He adds: "This is only the beginning of this process." He leaves, and I stay there in the cage, I don't know how long.

After a while, they come back for me. They put me in a capsule, some type of a spacecraft. Everything is automatic. There are a lot of flashing lights. I'm alone. I feel that the capsule starts to shake very hard. It is shaking and shaking. I feel a tremendous thrust in some direction. I realize now that I'm flying in this capsule. After a while, not too long, there is a big bang. Then a few more bangs, everything tumbles, and then everything stops. The capsule splits in two. I find myself in a strange place where I've never been. There is a lot of green. I look around and decide to move away, to see where I am. While I'm moving, I notice that I'm very small relative to other things there.

A: *Is it not normal for you to be small?*

B: No. I see other creatures like myself, only they don't have hands. There are all these creatures. I try to communicate with them, but I'm not successful.

A: Using words or thoughts?

B: Both. It seems they have no ability to communicate with me. I can make all kinds of sounds, but it seems they can't. I feel a great loneliness. I decide to get moving, but first I want to see the capsule, to see what condition it's in. Maybe I can fly away, but it looks pretty hopeless. It was split in half, and it looks burnt. I don't think it's going to go anywhere. I decide to get moving. I move slowly because I have no energy. Everything is big, all that green. I don't know what I'm supposed to do here. For some reason they wanted me to be here, so I don't ask too many questions. I assume they will come back for me sometime. I move forward, and it seems I'm getting out of the green. I reach an area that is more gray or brown. There are many large things moving around. Everything looks huge and scary. I feel so insignificant, like I have no importance at all, compared to all those huge things. I don't understand why I feel insignificant, maybe because I'm very vulnerable, and they can step on me. Suddenly, I find myself in a gray area where there are a lot of big things moving around, and I want to find the green again. I can't find it, and I keep moving. Suddenly, I feel a strong thump. I was probably killed. I was just stepped on and killed.

A: What happens next?

B: I went back to what I was before the spacecraft. I'm taken down the hallway again, the opposite direction from before. Now there are also creatures in the windows. I'm not afraid. I get to the commander. There is no communication between us, just an understanding. There is an understanding that I'm happier than I was before.

A: Has anything else changed?

B: No.

A: Do you do the same work you did before?

B: Yes.

A: May I speak with Ben's Mediator?

Mediator: Yes.

A: Why did you choose to show Ben this life today?

M: To demonstrate that everything is relative. Even if he is not happy, it could be worse, so it's preferable to be happy.

A: *Is that the same lesson that his commander wanted him to learn in that life?*

M: Yes. He felt insignificant when he was little. I wanted to show him that everyone is equally important, no matter what size he or she is. It's all about feelings and nothing else. Everyone is a lot of things, not just what he seems to be at the moment.

A: *Are you talking about people or everything?*

M: Everything.

A: *Everything in the universe?*

M: Yes.

A: *When you say everyone is many things, do you mean in terms of character, or are they actually a lot of things, creatures?*

M: They are really a lot of things, one thing right now and then something else.

A: *So even when he was a cockroach, he should not have felt insignificant?*

M: Right.

A: *How does that relate to his life now?*

M: He feels unimportant sometimes when he compares himself to other people.

A: *What was the meaning of him having hands when he was a cockroach?*

M: It was to remind him where he came from. So that he would ask himself questions and not get absorbed by the world. To not miss the experience, that lesson, and give meaning to what he is.

A: *Is there anything parallel to that in his life now as Ben?*

M: He sees all kinds of people that are "important", and he doesn't feel that he is also important. He asks himself why he is not like them. He needs to be reminded that he is.

A: *So are you saying that in fact, to some extent, he is being absorbed by this world, by this world's standards?*

M: Yes.

A: *Maybe it's related; Ben asks how he could be more positive.*

M: He should remember that positivity is also possible, and he shouldn't get absorbed into negativity. He should focus on the positive, not on the negative; focus on his hands and not on his "cockroach".

A: *It sounds easy in theory, but how can he put it into practice?*

M: He has to be mindful of his negative thoughts and his automatic behavior. He has to stop himself and think, not just respond reflexively.

A: *Is he so used to negative thinking that it has become automatic, a habit, and he doesn't even notice?*

M: Yes. He should be more open to things and not dismiss them offhand. He should say more yes than no, if he wants to enjoy life more.

COMMENTARY

In this session Ben was not happy with his life and this had consequences. He was shown that things could be worse, and that helped him to appreciate his life more. He learned that it was better to focus on the positive and not the negative.

MESSAGES

1. Everything is relative. Things could always be worse.
2. Everyone is equally important.
3. Do not get absorbed into negativity. Positivity is always possible.
4. To have more positive experiences, say 'yes' more often than 'no.'

STUDY QUESTIONS

1. What positive aspects of yourself or your life could you focus on, to be happier?
2. In what situations, if any, do you consider yourself less important than others?
3. Do you tend to stop the flow of your life by saying no to opportunities?

AFFIRMATIONS

1. I appreciate myself and all good things in my life, so I feel happy and fulfilled.
2. I am excited about opportunities that show up in my life and eager to try new things.

SESSION TWENTY-TWO

Parting with Perfection

THIS session was also conducted during my visit in Israel. Ben wanted to know if the universe was infinite.

Ben: I'm on grass. I'm some kind of colored squares made of smoke, dense smoke. I see other squares. They're all moving. There are big brown arrows on the ground. They're all following the arrows. I'm also following the arrows.

Anat: Are they all moving in the same direction?

B: No. There are different tracks. Each one has his own route. They are not switching between tracks.

A: What does it feel like being there?

B: There are no feelings or thoughts.

A: Does the track have an end?

B: It goes somewhere.

A: So move forward in time until you get to where you're supposed to.

B: I move along this track, and at the end there is a huge screen made of lots of colors. I see everyone else going into it. I'm going into it too. I'm entering it right now.

A: What happens when you do?

B: I simply exit it. I'm off to another lane.

A: Does it look the same as the previous track?

B: No. It's as if I am not what I was before. I look similar to before, but with slightly different colors and a slightly different size.

A: Do you feel different?

B: Yes. I am something else apparently. I have no additional knowledge or anything. I know I'm different; I'm not what I was before.

A: *How do you feel about that?*

B: I don't have a feeling. I'm following a track and know that at the end of the track I'll get back to the screen. I reach the screen and merge with all those colors. It's like a three-dimensional screen, like a giant rectangle of colors. Translucent colors, and I'm part of it now.

A: *What does it feel like to be a part of it?*

B: It feels kind of perfect.

A: *Are there any thoughts?*

B: There are no thoughts because everything is perfect. There is no need for thoughts.

A: *And then what happens?*

B: I know I need to part with this perfection.

A: *Why?*

B: Because it's boring.

A: *So what happens?*

B: I leave the screen. I leave in order to go back.

A: *Go back where?*

B: To forget maybe. Forget the perfection, as if to reach perfection again.

A: *Do you get out?*

B: I'm out. I'm over this turf, over the grass. There are arrows on the ground, but I don't follow them. Others follow the arrows. I'm free. I'm moving in different directions. Sometimes I follow the arrows, and then I get off the tracks. I move freely.

A: *Is there a feeling when you move?*

B: No.

A: *Thoughts?*

B: There are thoughts. Where should I go?

A: *And how do you decide where to go?*

B: I just move in different directions, where I want, without any restrictions. There is a feeling of freedom, but with it a feeling of lack of direction, lack of purpose. I know I need to reach perfection, so I'm moving and looking for arrows. I think that only with the arrows I will get to perfection. But every time I follow a track, I can't reach perfection. I can't reach the screen. That's how I keep going and don't succeed.

A: *How do you feel all this time when you don't succeed?*

B: Probably some frustration. Helplessness.

A: *What happens next?*

B: I find myself moving in different directions instead of following the tracks. I notice that if I concentrate, I can create arrows on the ground and move them. I feel good. It feels right. I follow the arrows I create. When I follow them, I reach the rectangle screen. Then I once again merge with the colors and achieve perfection.

A. *Do you stay there?*

B: Yes, I do.

A: *And then what?*

B: I am just complete. Nothing is happening.

A: *Are you staying there in that perfection?*

B: Yes, until I leave it again.

A: *Because it's boring? Or is there another reason?*

B: Yes, it's a little boring.

A: *What happens when you leave again?*

B: The same thing. Once again I move in different directions. Again I create arrows and get back to perfection.

A: *What is it like to be in that perfection?*

B: Like everything and nothing at the same time, like one big paradox. There is something incomplete; something is missing in this perfection.

A: *What is missing in the perfection?*

B: Movement is missing.

A: *Is that something you understand now, that you are inside the perfection?*

B: Yes.

A: *Do you decide anything about that?*

B: That there is no choice; I have to get out of the perfection and then return to it, again and again. It's like energy, a type of polarity. There is always a circular motion between the poles. Everything is in motion. Even perfection needs movement, you have to leave and then reach it again.

A: *Can't movement exist inside the perfection?*

B: No. Movement can only exist where there is no perfection.

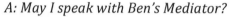

A: May I speak with Ben's Mediator?

Mediator: Yes.

A: Why did you show him this scenario today?

M: To make him realize that no matter which way he goes, as long as it's *his* way, he will reach perfection. Perfection is not a goal. The goal is the path to perfection. The goal is your path.

A: Is his goal to find his path and follow it?

M: His goal is to understand that whatever path he follows, as long as it is *his* path, it is the way to perfection. He has to accept his path and know that whatever he does is right for him. Instead, he looks at other paths.

A: Of other people?

M: Yes.

A: What happens when he looks at other paths?

M: He doesn't follow his own path and doesn't reach perfection.

A: Is it like following arrows that are not his, in this story?

M: Yes. He should create his own arrows and lay them down where he moves.

A. What prevents him from doing that?

M: Insecurity, fear, jealousy.

A: Envying other people and their paths?

M: Yes. He should understand that the arrows are what's important, not perfection. It doesn't matter where the arrows are, as long as they are his. No matter where they lead, it is the right way.

A: Is he aware of what his path is?

M: Not yet. He needs to find it.

A: Will he?

M: Yes. Everyone does.

A. And perfection is not the goal?

M: Right. There is no perfection. Perfection is the path to perfection.

A: Ben wants to know if the universe is infinite.

M: Yes, it is. There is nothing other than the universe.

A: *And parallel universes? You said before that there are parallel universes.*

M: Yes, but there is nothing else besides.

A: *Is there anything that this information contributes to us?*

M: That there are infinite possibilities.

A: *In life?*

M: Yes.

A: *What does that mean on a small scale, in regard to our lives?*

M: That we could do a lot more things than we think we could.

A: *Do we limit ourselves?*

M: Yes.

A: *Why do we tend to limit ourselves?*

M: Because we see ourselves as finite, as the same all the time. We look at ourselves in the mirror and see the same thing all the time.

A: *But we are actually changing.*

M: Yes, but in our perception we are the same. It makes our thinking limited and not as infinite as it could be. We are constantly reminded of who we are, and that limits us.

A: *Who we are — do you mean our human identity?*

M: Yes. We can remind ourselves that even if our human identity is one-dimensional, our thought is endless. We can do infinite things.

A: *Ben also asks what happens on other planets.*

M: Other planets have similar limitations. Beings limit themselves, although they are infinite in various ways.

A: *Those limitations, are they like the decision to part with perfection?*

M: The decision to leave perfection is an endless decision. It is an infinite understanding that there is no perfection.

A: *Where do these limitations come from?*

M: From the illusion that we are finite and limited.

A. *Did we choose to live in this illusion?*

M: Yes, so that we can attain perfection through it. Because if we were not in the illusion, we would be in perfection, then it would be boring. The illusion causes movement.

A: *Is the illusion a result of the decision to leave perfection?*

M: Yes.

A: So basically, going back to perfection is to remember and understand that we are infinite?

M: Yes.

A: I have a question. Why is it difficult for Ben to conduct these sessions?

M: It will be easier when Ben understands that this is part of his life and not something separate. It's an experience like any other experience.

A: Why does he think it's a separate experience?

M: It feels less natural for him than his everyday life. When he realizes that it is natural, it will be easier. It's a matter of awareness, understanding and acceptance of the change in consciousness. When he enters hypnosis, it's as real as the rest of his experiences.

A: Does he still doubt that it's real?

M: It's not about being real; it's about his perception of it. It is an experience like any other experience of life and as real.

COMMENTARY

In this session there is a description of consciousness that is following a path toward perfection. In the end, perfection is reached, but since it is boring without movement, perfection is left behind. Then the process repeats itself.

MESSAGES

1. As long as you follow your own path, it is the right way regardless of where it leads.
2. Perfection is not the goal.
3. There are infinite possibilities in life.

STUDY QUESTIONS

1. Do you compare your path in life to others' paths and allow them to affect your choices?
2. How would your life be different if you knew you were infinite, and there were infinite possibilities?

AFFIRMATIONS

1. I am unique, and I allow my own heart to guide me on my life's journey.
2. I am limitless in my ability to experience and embrace life.

SESSION TWENTY-THREE

Hovering Skeletons

THIS session was conducted during another visit to Israel; a couple of years had passed since the previous session. By then, Ben had changed jobs and wanted to know if he should take on more responsibility at work.

Ben: I see black all around. It's cold. I look like a skeleton. I'm hovering. I'm descending into the black. I could stop, but I don't want to stop; I want to continue moving forward. I arrive at a large net. I see skeletons smeared there, smeared on the net. I try to go through the net and manage somehow. There are other nets there, which I'm trying to pass. Each net has more skeletons smeared on it; those that failed to get through. They are broken. I see hands, feet, skulls. They are all dispersed on the nets. I manage to pass through.

Anat: How do you feel after you managed to get through the nets?

B: I don't feel anything. I'm hovering and I see other skeletons hovering. I don't know what they are doing. The skeletons are starting to approach me. They try to take my hand and pull me. Initially, I manage to resist. But then one of them grabs my hand. We are flying very fast. He takes me and brings me to the large nets and shows me a lot of smeared skeletons I've seen before. He's trying to tell me that I'm not like them; I'm still whole. I'm not smeared there on the net.

A: Why is he telling you this?

B: I don't know. I don't know what his motives are. I feel bad for the other smeared skeletons. I survived, so I feel bad. I'm not the only survivor, but I'm among the survivors. I constantly see more skeletons crashing into the net. Some are trying to pass and succeed. Others are trying to pass and break.

A: *Is the other skeleton still with you?*

B: No. I'm just hovering in this black. I don't know what all this black is. It's some kind of nothing. Nothing that is all black.

A: *Move forward in time until something happens.*

B: I find myself holding a knife. I try to hit the other skeletons and dismantle them. I manage to hit them, but it doesn't help. I can't break them. They survive it. There is a sound when the knife hits the bones, but it doesn't do too much.

A: *How do the other skeletons react?*

B: They are indifferent, as if I'm not there. I feel scared, like I have to do it so they would not harm me. I don't know why I think they would hurt me, but I do. I decide to leave. I throw the knife away, toss it. I continue floating down somewhere. Gradually there are fewer and fewer skeletons. I go through all kinds of fire rings, fire screens.

A: *Doesn't the fire hurt you?*

B: It hurts me, but not significantly. I manage to get through and see all kinds of burned skeletons and fragments of burned skeletons. I get to a place that is not black but a shade of gray.

A: *Are there skeletons?*

B: Yes, there are hovering skeletons. They are not doing much. I'm waiting for someone to come and get me, but no one does. I see that all those skeletons are focused on themselves and don't care about anything. At least by their movements and their behavior... They each hover in their own territory, their way, their track. There are no interactions between them.

A: *So what do you decide to do?*

B: I decide to take a knife and hurt them again. Here I am successful. I hit them and they break. As I break more I feel safer, more confident they will not harm me. I decide to continue after I feel confident enough to move on. I continue hovering.

A: *Where are you headed?*

B: It seems that now I'm a butterfly. I jump from tree to tree.

A: *What does it feel like to be a butterfly?*

B: Stressful because I have to constantly move, jump and fly.

A: *Are there other butterflies around?*

B: I don't know. I'm not paying attention.

A: And then what happens?

B: I continue as a skeleton. There is dirt around me. I'm buried in the ground.

A: What happens next?

B: I'm a skeleton hovering. I arrive at a blue space, not black, dark blue. Here I see skeletons hovering, and I do see some interactions between them. Some go hand in hand.

A: How do you feel?

B: I feel good, and it feels right that there is interaction. The skeletons here aren't trying to hurt one another. I see that I'm holding a knife again. I'm debating whether to use it or not. I don't want them to hurt me. I don't want to take the risk; maybe someone will hurt me there. Yet I don't use the knife.

I go back to the cloud now.

A: May I speak to Ben's Mediator?

Mediator: Yes.

A: Why did you show him that he was a skeleton in a black space?

M: To make him understand that in the end he remains himself, his origin, his essence. His skeleton is his essence; it represents his infinite consciousness that is unique.

A: And why did you choose to show it as a skeleton?

M: Because it's something that is easy to understand. It's easy to imagine a skeleton. All other skeletons are also... The interaction is significant because the skeleton communicates, the essence communicates, not the masks and the covers.

A: So the skeleton represents the true essence under the mask, under the identity as a person?

M: Yes. It doesn't matter what his name is, what he does. What communicates is the essence.

A: What does the black space signify?

M: That there is nothing outside the essence of the skeleton. The other things do not really exist.

A: What is the meaning of the nets the skeletons had to go through?

M: It means that anyone, who doesn't realize that he is an essence, breaks. It's like he does not exist. His existence is destroyed if he doesn't understand that everything is himself. Everything is the skeleton, the other skeletons. As long as he doesn't see it, he shatters. When he realizes that, he is able to pass.

A: *How does this relate to life as a human? What does this mean about life?*

M: People focus on many unimportant things and events in life. The only thing that is significant is the interaction between essences, between awarenesses, and not everything that happens around them.

A: *When a skeleton came and took him by the hand to show him the nets, what did the skeleton want him to see?*

M: He wanted to show Ben that anyone, who does not understand what's important in life, breaks. Actually the skeleton showed him previous incarnations that broke.

A: *So in past lives they did not understand?*

M: Right. Then at some point there is an incarnation in which they understand, and they make it through the net.

A: *Why did he feel bad when he saw the other skeletons smeared, while he himself got through?*

M: Because those who failed to pass, he could not show them, could not help them figure out what would make them succeed in making it through. He felt bad because of it.

A: *Why couldn't he show them?*

M: Because it's something that is impossible to show. Only after you get through, you can look back and understand, but not before.

A: *Then he found himself holding a knife, and he tried to hurt the other skeletons. He was afraid of them. What does this mean?*

M: He was afraid they would hurt him and take him back.

A: *Was it possible to take him back?*

M: No, but he didn't know that.

A: *Then he tossed the knife and went through rings of fire. What is the significance of the fire?*

M: The fire symbolizes cleanliness, a complete purification of consciousness.

A: There he saw burned-out skeletons. He got through, but others were burned. Why did some get burned?

M: He moved quickly through the fire. Others moved more slowly to purify themselves. They tried to forget their essence.

A: Using the fire?

M: Yes.

A: Why did they try to forget their essence?

M: They wanted to be so pure as to diminish their existence, and that is not possible. This means that when you want to be too pure, you forget who and what you are, your essence.

A: So he moved faster and thus became more pure, but also kept his essence?

M: Yes.

A: Then he arrived at a gray space. There were skeletons, but there was no interaction between them. What does it mean?

M: That the skeletons processed what they had learned. It represents a stage of understanding.

A: And then there is no need to interact?

M: No. They need to understand what's happening, so they meditate.

A: Then he took a knife again. He decided to hurt them and was able to break them. Why?

M: Because they were exposed. They were at a stage of understanding and acceptance and were exposed to many things, and one of those things was being hurt by others. He tried to hurt them because it was part of the process he had to go through, the understanding that he could hurt them. If there is complete acceptance, beings are exposed, vulnerable and can be harmed.

A: Is there a parallel for this in human life?

M: Yes. If someone accepts you and loves you, hurting them becomes very easy.

A: The more he hurt them, the more confident he felt that they wouldn't hurt him. Why?

M: He was under the illusion that if he hurts others, he cannot be harmed.

A: But that's not true?

M: No.

A: *Then he became a butterfly. Why?*

M: To show him that even something as short-lived and light as a butterfly has an essence. It fulfills its role. It flies from tree to tree.

A: *Then he was a skeleton buried underground. What does this imply?*

M: That he is part of the ground, part of reality. On Earth he is part of the ground, part of Earth, in the end. He is part of the essence. All the skeletons came from the same place; all are connected to Earth.

A: *Then he arrived at the blue space as a skeleton. Among the skeletons there was interaction and nobody tried to hurt one another. What does this mean?*

M: When there is complete understanding, this is what happens. There is interaction and only acceptance and no harm. This is actually the goal.

A: *The goal of what?*

M: Of all essences. This goal can be achieved only with a complete understanding of the process. The understanding that everything is essence and interactions.

A: *Ben has a question. He asks if he should take on more responsibility at work.*

M: Yes, he should.

A: *What holds him back?*

M: The fear of what other people will think of him.

A: *If he fails?*

M: Yes.

A: *Is it related to what you showed him today, the skeletons?*

M: Yes, because what matters at the end is the essence and the interaction. To take on more responsibility means more interaction.

A: *Could you ease his fear of taking that step? What can you say about it?*

M: Not to worry.

COMMENTARY

This session describes the process of learning and understanding we go through in our various incarnations. It is described in a simplified and symbolic way. The skeletons represent pure consciousness, demonstrating that besides awareness and interactions, nothing is really important.

MESSAGES

1. Your unique essence remains forever.
2. Only the essence truly exists.
3. The idea that if you hurt others, you cannot be harmed, is an illusion.
4. The goal is acceptance through the understanding that everything is essence and interactions.

STUDY QUESTIONS

1. Are you able to recognize which aspects of your life are truly important?
2. Do you sometimes think you can protect yourself by hurting others?

AFFIRMATIONS

1. I am constantly improving my understanding of life and the purpose of living.
2. I enjoy the company of others because I see the magnificence of their essence.

SESSION TWENTY-FOUR

A Hidden Colony

THIS last session was conducted during the same visit in Israel. Ben had a cold and was not feeling well. He agreed to conduct the session, regardless.

Ben: I'm a man swimming. I'm in the middle of the ocean alone, somewhere. I don't know where I am. It's a little stressful.

Anat: Is there no one else there?

B: There is nothing. I'm floating in the water alone; half my body is in the water.

A: Is it day or night?

B: It's sunny and there are some waves. I don't know what's in the water.

A: Can you see into the water?

B: It's not clear at all. I'm trying, but I can't see. I don't know how I got here.

A: Move back in time until it becomes clear to you how you got there.

B: I'm on a jet ski. I'm riding my jet ski in the sea, and suddenly I run out of gas, so I stop and stay on the jet. I'm alone. I feel like I have to get off the jet ski. For some reason I feel that if I'm part of the sea, I'm safer. I get off the jet ski and let it go. I'm floating in the water. It seems I've been here for a few hours.

A: Move forward in time until something happens.

B: After a day or so, I suddenly feel a pull from under the water. It doesn't seem dangerous; it doesn't feel like sharks or anything like that. I feel more pulls... I'm trying to look down, but I can't see anything. Then suddenly I'm being pulled hard, and I'm going into the water. I'm able to breathe, to my surprise. I breathe, and something is pulling me. It's hard for me to see in the water. I'm being pulled toward the bottom, down, down. At first it's stressful, and then somehow I flow with it. I get really deep, where there is no light. I'm being pulled more and more, deeper and deeper.

A: *Can you see what is pulling you?*

B: I can't see. Everything is black. This black suddenly becomes less black, becomes gray, very dark gray, and gradually lighter and lighter. I'm still being pulled, and I'm deep down. Then the gray becomes whiter, and then I start to see the bottom. It looks like sand. As I get closer to the bottom, suddenly I'm pulled into a hole in the ground. Gradually, I begin to see what's pulling me. It looks like some sort of a fish, a fish with hands.

A: *Human hands?*

B: Something like that. I don't know how many fingers he has.

A: *Is the fish bigger than you?*

B: No. It's about my size.

A: *What else do you see?*

B: I see all kinds of fish swimming there, fish with hands.

A: *Do they have colors?*

B: Sort of green and black. They are not talking to each other; they are just swimming there. I'm trying to understand why they brought me here. I have no idea why that fish dragged me down.

A: *Are the fish paying attention to you?*

B: No, they are not interacting with me.

A: *What are you doing there? Standing? Swimming?*

B: I'm kind of swimming, diving.

A: *Can you breathe in the water?*

B: Yes.

A: *Do you see other people there or just fish?*

B: Only those fish.

A: *Move forward in time until something happens, or until you figure out why you are there.*

B: I realize that these fish came to Earth some time ago. They originally came as humans, but they couldn't be human, so they became fish.

A: *Why couldn't they be human?*

B: Because they were persecuted.

A: *Who persecuted them?*

B: Humans who had been on Earth before them, because they looked a little different.

A: *So they hide from humans?*

B: They hide, yes, from humans.

A: *What do you think of that?*

B: I'm angry that they were persecuted because they were a little different.

A: *Where did they come from?*

B: They came from a different planet which died. They could not live there anymore.

A: *Do you know how they managed to become fish?*

B: They started to build a colony underwater. They couldn't breathe underwater, so they used instruments. They gradually tried to breathe without instruments until after about 5,000 years, they succeeded. They adapted to living underwater. Their body changed, and they became more like fish than humans. They still had human hands and eyes, and a head that looked human. Not exactly like fish, not exactly like humans.

A: *How can you breathe underwater?*

B: I don't know how. It's strange. It took them 5,000 years, and I just got here.

A: *Can you communicate with them?*

B: Yes, by thinking. I read their thoughts.

A: *Ask them how you're able to breathe in the water.*

B: They say that they attached strips to my leg that provide oxygen through the skin.

A: *Ask them why they brought you there.*

B: To show me what it's like for them here. To show me that there are things on Earth which we, humans, don't see. That what happened to them was because of people and human society.

A: *Why is it important to show you that?*

B: It is not important to show *me*; I just happened to be there.

A: *But why is it important for them to show it to someone?*

B: Because they want to get out of the water, and they don't know how by now. They need someone to help them. They think maybe, if there is a small chance they can explain their story, people will accept them. Something like that... It's boring for them in the water. It's also very dangerous with all kinds of animals that people don't even know about. It happened that these human fish got taken and eaten. They believe it would be less dangerous for them on land if only humanity accepted them.

A: How do you respond to that?

B: I don't know what to tell them. Am I supposed to tell people about them? I don't know what to do.

A: Don't you want to tell people about them?

B: I don't know how.

A: Ask them.

B: They don't know either. They don't have answers; they have questions. They don't really know what to do. They got into a situation they did not want to be in.

A: Is there anything else you want to ask them, or they want to tell you?

B: Why did they choose Earth?

A: Ask them.

B: They say it was the planet closest to them, and it was relatively easy to reach.

A: Are they the only survivors of their planet?

B: No. They don't know what happened to the others. They only know that they escaped from the planet. Not all of them were trying to reach Earth. They don't know what happened to the others.

A: So what happens next? Do you get out of the water?

B: Yes, at some point I get out of the water.

A: Did they let you go?

B: Yes. I manage to get to the beach I came from.

A: Then what do you do?

B: I try to think about what I saw. I'm sad. I have sad thoughts... They're there for no good reason.

A: Do you decide to do something about it?

B: I don't know what to do.

A: Move forward in time until something happens, or until you decide something.

B: I decide to go to the cloud.

A: May I speak to Ben's Mediator?

Mediator: Yes.

A: Why did you show him that experience with the fish in the water?

M: So that he would know that the world, Earth, is worse than he thinks. Bad things happen that people don't even know about.

A: Why is it important for him to know that?

M: So that he will be a good person and teach his children to be good. Contribute to the good part of humanity. The power of evil is far greater than the power of good.

A: The power of evil is greater than the power of good? Do you mean on Earth?

M: Yes.

A: Then in the session today, after he got out of the water, did he decide to do anything with the information he got?

M: No, he did not.

A: How did he feel about it?

M: He regretted it, but he didn't know what else to do.

A: What was he supposed to do?

M: He should have perhaps told their story to others; and that might have made a difference.

A: Is this experience relevant to our book?

M: Yes, the book can make people a little kinder.

COMMENTARY

This session tells about an entire species of intelligent beings, who were forced to change their existence as a result of human bigotry and violence. They could not live on Earth's surface and were forced into hiding in the sea. They thought that thousands of years were enough time for humans to evolve enough to accept them. What do you think?

MESSAGES

1. There is much malevolence on Earth that people are not even aware of.
2. It is very important to be a kind person and contribute to the good part of humanity.

STUDY QUESTIONS

1. What would you have done with that information? Would you have tried to tell the story?
2. What are some possible ways to contribute to the good part of humanity?

AFFIRMATIONS

1. Because I value and accept myself, I value and accept all other beings and life forms.
2. I have the power to make a difference with my positive attitude and kind behavior.

To the Reader

My quest for the meaning of life led me to the creation of this book. I feel privileged and honored to be able to share with you the answers revealed to me during my work with Ben.

When we first started having these sessions, I couldn't imagine that they would one day become a book. Gradually, I came to realize that the insights revealed in the sessions could make a difference in people's lives. In the last session, Ben had an opportunity to make a difference and perhaps set free an entire species of intelligent beings. In that life he chose not to take action. However, he did eventually reveal the information, I believe, in a different incarnation, in the form of this book. It occurred to me that the last session could be viewed as a call to action. I see this book as an opportunity to reach out to people and share its wisdom in the hope that it will help them connect more deeply with their own selves and with others.

Understanding our deep and eternal connection to each other opens the door to unconditional love. It seems that true and pure love requires integrity and self-esteem. Genuine self-love means loving others and the world as well. When we love, honor, and respect ourselves, we naturally feel the same for others. We wish for others what we wish for ourselves. It is my hope that the messages in this book inspire you as they have inspired me.

Since we are all parts of one consciousness, there is no actual separation between one person to another, regardless of the current incarnation's narrative. I truly believe that as more and more people realize this simple truth, the better and more peaceful life here on Earth will be. Therefore, it is my deep desire that we all reach out to others and spread the word. When we all share these messages with our families, friends, neighbors, coworkers, we help pave the way to a better world, where we are all awakened to our true nature as kind and loving human beings.

Acknowledgments

I am deeply thankful to "Ben" for his willingness to close his eyes and open his mind in order to bring to life the information in this book. Obviously, without him and his cooperation this book would not have been possible.

I thank my parents, Judith and Freddy, my brother Eran, and my sister Leora, for their support and creative suggestions on how to make this book better.
My sincere thank you goes to Judith Weinstein for the many hours spent on editing.

I would like to express my appreciation to the "Hypnotherapy Academy of America" and to Dolores Cannon (1931-2014), whose workshop I attended, for the excellent education I received.

I wish to express my deepest gratitude to Anna Paderna for investing her time and efforts in improving this book.

Special thanks to Digital Donna for the great artwork on the cover. It was a real pleasure working with her.

I am also grateful to Johnny Miller for his creative suggestions.

In addition, there are several people, whose names are not mentioned, and who made meaningful contributions to the creation of this book.